Hebrews

Back to the Bible Study Guides

HEBREWS

OUR SUPERIOR SAVIOR

WOODROW KROLL

CROSSWAY BOOKS
WHEATON, ILLINOIS

Hebrews: Our Superior Savior

Copyright © 2008 by Back to the Bible

Published by Crossway Books
           a publishing ministry of Good News Publishers
           1300 Crescent Street
           Wheaton, Illinois 60187

Cover photo: iStock

First printing, 2008

Printed in the United States of America

ISBN 13: 978-1-4335-0126-5
ISBN 10: 1-4335-0126-0

Unless otherwise indicated, all Scripture quotations are taken from *The Holy Bible: English Standard Version*®. Copyright © 2001 by Crossway Bibles, a publishing ministry of Good News Publishers. Used by permission. All rights reserved.

Produced with the assistance of The Livingstone Corporation (www.LivingstoneCorp.com).

Project Staff: Neil Wilson

CH		18	17	16	15	14	13	12	11	10	09	08
15	14	13	12	11	10	9	8	7	6	5	4	3	2	1

Table of Contents

How to Use This Study

The entire text of Hebrews from the English Standard Version is printed before each day's devotional reading, so that everything you need is in one place. While we recommend reading the Scripture passage before you read the devotional, some have found it helpful to use the devotional as preparation for reading the Scripture. If you are unfamiliar with the English Standard Version (on which this series of studies is based), you might consider reading the included Bible selection, then the devotional, then the passage again from a different Bible translation with which you are more comfortable or familiar. This will give you an excellent biblical preparation for considering the rest of the lesson.

After each devotional there are three sections designed to help you better understand and apply the lesson's Scripture passage.

Consider It—Several questions that will give you a better understanding of the Scripture passage for the day. These could be used for a small group discussion.

Express It—Suggestions for turning the insights from the lesson into prayer.

Go Deeper—Throughout this study you will benefit from seeing how the Letter to the Hebrews fits with the rest of the Bible. This additional section will include other passages and insights from Scripture. The Go Deeper section will also allow you to consider some of the implications of the day's passage for the central theme of the study—our superior Savior—as well as other key Scripture themes.

The Superiority of Jesus

The world often claims today that one savior is just as good as another. The world is wrong. Why look for a "just-as-good" savior when there is One who is the best (and only) Savior?

Hebrews 1:1–14

The Supremacy of God's Son

1 Long ago, at many times and in many ways, God spoke to our fathers by the prophets, ²but in these last days he has spoken to us by his Son, whom he appointed the heir of all things, through whom also he created the world. ³He is the radiance of the glory of God and the exact imprint of his nature, and he upholds the universe by the word of his power. After making purification for sins, he sat down at the right hand of the Majesty on high, ⁴having become as much superior to angels as the name he has inherited is more excellent than theirs.

⁵For to which of the angels did God ever say,

> "You are my Son,
>   today I have begotten you"?

Or again,

> "I will be to him a father,
>   and he shall be to me a son"?

⁶And again, when he brings the firstborn into the world, he says,

> "Let all God's angels worship
>   him."

⁷Of the angels he says,

> "He makes his angels winds,
>   and his ministers a flame of
>   fire."

⁸But of the Son he says,

> "Your throne, O God, is forever
>   and ever,
>   the scepter of uprightness is
>   the scepter of your
>   kingdom.

⁹You have loved righteousness
>   and hated wickedness;
> therefore God, your God, has
>   anointed you
> with the oil of gladness
>   beyond your
>   companions."

¹⁰And,

> "You, Lord, laid the foundation of
>   the earth in the
>   beginning,
>   and the heavens are the work
>   of your hands;
> ¹¹they will perish, but you remain;
>   they will all wear out like a
>   garment,
> ¹²like a robe you will roll them up,
>   like a garment they will be
>   changed.
> But you are the same,
>   and your years will have no
>   end."

¹³And to which of the angels has he ever said,

> "Sit at my right hand
>   until I make your enemies a
>   footstool for your feet"?

¹⁴Are they not all ministering spirits sent out to serve for the sake of those who are to inherit salvation?

Key Verse

He is the radiance of the glory of God and the exact imprint of his nature, and he upholds the universe by the word of his power. After making purification for sins, he sat down at the right hand of the Majesty on high (Heb. 1:3).

Go Deeper

From a recent Barna Group survey, it was determined that 75 percent of Americans believe that angels are real. God's Word tells us a lot about angels. Angels are persons. They're not *its* or things. There are so many of them you can't count them—thousands, ten thousands, ten thousands times ten thousands! Angels are powerful beings. They can do things we cannot do. They are intelligent beings—certainly smarter and more aware than we are. They function more directly in God's presence than we do. But just because they're superior to humans doesn't mean angels are superior to everyone. Angels are not superior to Jesus.

Perhaps your Bible translates Hebrews 1:4 as "better than angels." "Better," "superior"—it's the same word.

Interestingly enough, that word *better* or *superior* occurs 13 times in this tiny Book of Hebrews. And the writer of Hebrews declares that everything about Jesus is superior.

Why is He superior to the angels? What is it that sets Him apart from angels in this world? Notice in verses 4–6 that there is a special relationship between Jesus and God the Father and a special relationship between Jesus and angels. To God, Jesus is Son. To angels, Jesus is One to be worshiped—God. This, by the way, answers those who believe that Jesus is or was an angel. That idea is nowhere found in Scripture. We don't pray to angels. They join us in praising and worshiping the Son of God. For a vivid description of this, read Revelation 5.

The Letter to the Hebrews comes to us with no human writer indicated. But the content of this New Testament book indicates eloquently the Holy Spirit's authorship. This is an important bridge document that makes the Old Testament come alive in a new way for followers of Jesus. Hebrews begins by reminding us that God had already been talking to His creation for a long time before "the Word became flesh and dwelt among us" (John 1:14). God spoke to our forefathers, says the writer of Hebrews, through the prophets; but now He is speaking to us through His Son, Jesus.

According to this first chapter of Hebrews, Jesus is superior as a communicator of God's Word. When compared to the two main types of messengers (prophets and angels), Jesus is in a class by Himself. The Old Testament prophets were called of God and spoke what God wanted communicated in their times and in many ways (see Heb. 1:1), but none of them had Jesus' credentials—the Son of God. Angelic servants of God had the same limitation despite their impressive appearance.

> **"'I count everything as loss because of the surpassing worth of knowing Christ Jesus my Lord' (Phil. 3:8). That describes a superior Savior!"**

Therefore Jesus is exalted over all the other ways God has communicated in the past. None of the Old Testament prophets—not Isaiah, not Jeremiah, not Daniel, not Ezekiel—could claim that he was the Son of God.

Jesus is unique. When it came to communicating God's will, He accomplished the same task that prophets and angels did, but He did it perfectly, completely. He is the Superior Communicator. He stands apart from all the rest of the world because, the Bible says, this particular prophet through whom God spoke had a relationship to God that no other Prophet ever had—the relationship as the Son of God. Even the genuine prophets were merely servants of God. Jesus is the Son of God.

While we're thinking about the superior position of Jesus, we have to add His role as God's chief executive officer "through whom [Jesus, God the Son] also he [God the Father] created the world" (Heb. 1:2). Jesus is God's heir when it comes to "all things" (v. 2). While on earth Jesus could heal humans, give orders to nature (tell a storm to quiet down), and overrule laws of nature (multiply bread and fish) because He knows how creation works. He set it up to begin with.

As the second person of the Godhead, the Son of God (John 3:16), Jesus, was in a superior position to do for His creation what angels could not do. Psalm 8 reminds us that we (and for a time Jesus) are a little lower than the angels. But angels are still created creatures like us; therefore, an angel couldn't die for us as a substitute, but Jesus could. In Jesus' divine portfolio, "after making purification for sins, he sat down at the right hand of the Majesty on high" (Heb. 1:3).

Jesus claimed to have a relationship with God that is unique and distinct. John the Baptist said of Jesus, "For he whom God has sent utters the words of God" (John 3:34). Jesus said about Himself, "If you knew me, you would know my Father also" (John 8:19) and "[I] speak just as the Father taught me" (John 8:28). So, the words that Jesus speaks are not words that were revealed to Him by God—He, the Son, actually is speaking the words of God the Father. That's a sharp distinction and a mark of superiority.

Micah spoke words revealed by God. Jeremiah spoke words revealed by God. The prophet Muhammad claimed to speak words revealed by Allah. But here's the difference: Jesus does not speak the words revealed to Him by Jehovah. Jesus knows the words of Jehovah. God simply speaks through Jesus. There is no revelation necessary because He knows the words of God. And only the Son of God can know the Word of God. So His position is unique and different from all the others.

We are titling this survey of Hebrews *Our Superior Savior* because that is the wonderful theme of the letter. The chapters we will study lift up candidate after candidate who merit our attention—angels, prophets, Melchizedek the high priest, great men and women of faith—all who ultimately must acknowledge, as we do, that Jesus is superior. Jesus' relationship to the Father is superior; His work is superior, and the offer He makes to us is superior to any other we could accept. He offers to us a relationship with Him and His Father that no one else could offer. Perhaps the apostle Paul put it as well as anyone when he wrote, "I count everything as loss because of the surpassing worth of knowing Christ Jesus my Lord" (Phil. 3:8). Now that describes a superior Savior!

Express It

Our mental image and our thoughts about Jesus can always be improved. Until we see Him face-to-face, we will always be looking through a "mirror dimly" (1 Cor. 13:12). Pray that as a result of your study of Hebrews you will experience in a new way the superiority and majesty of Jesus Christ.

Consider It

As you read Hebrews 1:1–14, consider these questions:

1) As you begin this study of Hebrews, what is your current impression of the purpose of the letter?

_____

_____

2) According to this chapter, who is Jesus?

_____

_____

3) How is God the Father distinguished from God the Son in these verses?

_____

_____

4) Whom do you find more impressive, a genuine prophet or an angel? Why?

_____

_____

5) How does this first chapter of Hebrews relate to what some people today believe about angels? What do you think is the source of people's knowledge about angels?

_____

_____

6) What would you say is a balanced and biblical view of angels and their role as God's messengers?

_____

_____

7) How do you acknowledge the superiority of Jesus in your own life?

_____

_____

8) What perspective does Hebrews 1:10–12 bring to those who think the central responsibility of human beings is to preserve the world?

_____

_____

Lesson

2

Why Is Jesus Superior?

A leader might be recognized by his title or his uniform. He might be acknowledged because someone speaks well of him. But a leader ultimately proves himself superior by what he does.

Hebrews 2:1–18

Warning Against Neglecting Salvation

2 Therefore we must pay much closer attention to what we have heard, lest we drift away from it. ²For since the message declared by angels proved to be reliable, and every transgression or disobedience received a just retribution, ³how shall we escape if we neglect such a great salvation? It was declared at first by the Lord, and it was attested to us by those who heard, ⁴while God also bore witness by signs and wonders and various miracles and by gifts of the Holy Spirit distributed according to his will.

The Founder of Salvation

⁵Now it was not to angels that God subjected the world to come, of which we are speaking. ⁶It has been testified somewhere,

> "What is man, that you are
> mindful of him,
> or the son of man, that you
> care for him?
> ⁷You made him for a little while
> lower than the angels;
> you have crowned him with
> glory and honor,
>
> ⁸putting everything in
> subjection under his feet."

Now in putting everything in subjection to him, he left nothing outside his control. At present, we do not yet see everything in subjection to him. ⁹But we see him who for a little while was made lower than the angels, namely Jesus, crowned with glory and honor because of the suffering of death, so that by the grace of God he might taste death for everyone.

¹⁰For it was fitting that he, for whom and by whom all things exist, in bringing many sons to glory, should make the founder of their salvation perfect through suffering. ¹¹For he who sanctifies and those who are sanctified all have one

---

Key Verse

But we see him who for a little while was made lower than the angels, namely Jesus, crowned with glory and honor because of the suffering of death, so that by the grace of God he might taste death for everyone (Heb. 2:9).

---

source. That is why he is not ashamed to call them brothers, ¹²saying,

> "I will tell of your name to my
> brothers;
> in the midst of the
> congregation I will sing
> your praise."

¹³And again,

> "I will put my trust in him."

And again,

> "Behold, I and the children God
> has given me."

¹⁴Since therefore the children share in flesh and blood, he himself likewise partook of the same things, that through death he might destroy the one who has the power of death, that is, the devil, ¹⁵and deliver all those who through fear of death were subject to lifelong slavery. ¹⁶For surely it is not angels that he helps, but he helps the offspring of Abraham. ¹⁷Therefore he had to be made like his brothers in every respect, so that he might become a merciful and faithful high priest in the service of God, to make propitiation for the sins of the people. ¹⁸For because he himself has suffered when tempted, he is able to help those who are being tempted.

Go Deeper

One of the purposes behind the Letter to the Hebrews is basic teaching and application. We must not only learn but also do. That purpose can be seen in the opening verses of chapter 2. We are told to "pay much closer attention" (Heb. 2:1) and then gently confronted with the question, "How shall we escape if we neglect such a great salvation?" (v. 3). Although he does not use the term, the writer urges us repeatedly to go deeper!

A series of passages in this letter can be an encouragement to us to pay attention and persevere in our faith. Read the following: 2:1–4; 3:1–2, 12–13; 4:11–16; 6:10–12; 10:19–39; 12:1–14. The life to which Jesus calls us can be called *rest* as we will see, but it's never called *coasting!*

The theme of escape that is mentioned in the second chapter comes up again in the next to last chapter: "See that you do not refuse him who is speaking. For if they did not escape when they refused him who warned them on earth, much less will we escape if we reject him who warns from heaven" (12:25). From our study of Jesus, *Our Superior Savior,* in Hebrews, we will learn about the only person who can make escape from sin and death possible. Our study provides us with daily assurance that we know the One who can help us persevere to the end.

The Boulder Dam (now known as the Hoover Dam) was built in order to bring water to the southwestern region of the United States and California, to desert areas that did not have any water. After the completion of the dam, a plaque was attached in memory of those who had given their lives during the building of that great project. The plaque says, "These died that the desert might rejoice and blossom as the rose." Some sacrificed that others might live. Their sacrifice also teaches us about the beauty and limits of sacrifice.

In chapter 2 of Hebrews, the writer continues to develop the case for Christ's superiority, particularly as it relates to angels. The question is whether any sacrifice an angel could make would, in any way, come close to the sacrifice that Jesus made. Can the sacrifice of a creature (angel, human, or animal) compare with Christ's sacrifice? Would any sacrifice Buddha made even come close to the sacrifice

> *"Jesus is the ultimate superior Person, the only God-man there will ever be, the only Savior this world will ever have. It's because He gave the only sacrifice that makes a difference."*

that Jesus made? Would any sacrifice that Muhammad or any other person who was a leader of a world religion make equal Christ's sacrificial death? No. Jesus' sacrifice was superior because it was a saving sacrifice.

The Scripture quote included in Hebrews 2:6–8 reminds us immediately of Psalm 8 with its powerful claims about humanity and about "the son of man" (see Ps. 8:4–6). These verses place humans just below the angels in the created order and then indicate that Someone above the angels was "for a little while lower than the angels" (Heb. 2:7). That Someone is Jesus, whom the angels worship. Jesus joined our lower status in order to fulfill perfectly His role as Savior in accordance with God's plan: "For it was fitting that he, for whom and by whom all things exist, in bringing many sons to glory, should make the founder of their salvation perfect through suffering" (v. 10). Jesus Himself didn't need to be made perfect, but His role as Savior could not be perfect (complete, nothing lacking) unless He fully identified Himself with us—became one of us. By His life, by His death, and by His Resurrection, Jesus proved Himself to be our perfect Savior.

This chapter of Hebrews reminds us that God brought salvation to mankind, but He did not entrust salvation to us. He did not say to you or me, "You are in charge of this whole earth. Figure out a way that you can atone for your sins and get back to Me." He knows we can't save ourselves, and He knows that angels can't save us either. It appears that angels have chosen up sides already. Both those who chose to remain faithful to God and those who chose to join in Lucifer's rebellion against God have sealed their destiny. They no longer need God's intervention—but we do. That's why we find in verse 16, "For surely it is not angels that he helps, but he helps the offspring of Abraham."

The Book of 1 Peter points out the limited roles both prophets and angels have had in the outworking of salvation: "It was revealed to them [prophets] that they were serving not themselves but you, in the things that have now been announced to you through those who preached the good news to you by the Holy Spirit sent from heaven, things into which angels long to look" (1 Pet. 1:12). This tells us the angels are anxious to look into, to investigate, to learn more about, and to understand what they cannot experience—our salvation. I don't know about you, but I don't want to trust my eternal salvation to beings who don't even understand it!

Jesus is the ultimate superior Person, the only God-man there will ever be, the only Savior this world will ever have. It's because He gave the only sacrifice that makes a difference. The fact that Jesus was willing to "taste death for everyone" (Heb. 2:9) allows us to see His perfection in two distinct ways. First, He endured death "for" us. Verse 17 describes this work "to make propitiation for the sins of the people," meaning Jesus settled the account or dealt with sin as it needed to be dealt with in order to bring us back to a right standing with God. Second, Jesus' death forces us to recognize His unique relationship with us as an ongoing Helper, "for because he himself has suffered when tempted, he is able to help those who are being tempted" (v. 18). Jesus not only demonstrated His superiority as our Savior on the cross, but He also demonstrates it as our merciful companion every day.

Express It

How do you see Jesus "crowned with glory and honor" (v. 9)? When you bow in prayer before Him, what words, titles, and attitudes let Him know that you are giving Him glory and honor? This chapter tells us that what Jesus did for us—and does for us—and gives us good reasons to worship Him.

Consider It

As you read Hebrews 2:1–18, consider these questions:

1) What kind of warning did the writer put at the beginning of this chapter?

_____

_____

_____

2) In what ways does this warning still apply to us?

_____

_____

_____

3) How does this chapter describe Jesus' present position and role? (See vv. 17–18).

_____

_____

_____

4) What was unique and superior about Jesus' death?

_____

_____

_____

5) In what ways is Jesus Christ like us?

_____

_____

_____

6) How does the fact that Jesus experienced all aspects of life and even tasted death affect your relationship with Him?

_____

_____

_____

7) In what situations or relationships do you need to keep reminding yourself that Jesus is fully aware of what's going on?

_____

_____

_____

Jesus' Faithfulness

When we identify someone as an example for us, we usually think in somewhat narrow terms. He or she represents what a father or mother should be, what a friend should be, what a teacher should be. We're about to look at an example that fits for all of life and every role, including that of savior.

Hebrews 3:1–19

Jesus Greater Than Moses

3 Therefore, holy brothers, you who share in a heavenly calling, consider Jesus, the apostle and high priest of our confession, ²who was faithful to him who appointed him, just as Moses also was faithful in all God's house. ³For Jesus has been counted worthy of more glory than Moses—as much more glory as the builder of a house has more honor than the house itself. ⁴(For every house is built by someone, but the builder of all things is God.) ⁵Now Moses was faithful in all God's house as a servant, to testify to the things that were to be spoken later, ⁶but Christ is faithful over God's house as a son. And we are his house if indeed we hold fast our confidence and our boasting in our hope.

> # Key Verse
>
> *But Christ is faithful over God's house as a son. And we are his house if indeed we hold fast our confidence and our boasting in our hope* (Heb. 3:6).

A Rest for the People of God

⁷Therefore, as the Holy Spirit says,

"Today, if you hear his voice,
⁸do not harden your hearts as in
the rebellion,
on the day of testing in the
wilderness,
⁹where your fathers put me to the
test
and saw my works for forty years.
¹⁰Therefore I was provoked with
that generation,
and said, 'They always go astray
in their heart;
they have not known my ways.'
¹¹As I swore in my wrath,
'They shall not enter my
rest.'"

¹²Take care, brothers, lest there be in any of you an evil, unbelieving heart, leading you to fall away from the living God. ¹³But exhort one another every day, as long as it is called "today," that none of you may be hardened by the deceitfulness of sin. ¹⁴For we have come to share in Christ, if indeed we hold our original confidence firm to the end. ¹⁵As it is said,

"Today, if you hear his voice,
do not harden your hearts as in
the rebellion."

¹⁶For who were those who heard and yet rebelled? Was it not all those who left Egypt led by Moses? ¹⁷And with whom was he provoked for forty years? Was it not with those who sinned, whose bodies fell in the wilderness? ¹⁸And to whom did he swear that they would not enter his rest, but to those who were disobedient? ¹⁹So we see that they were unable to enter because of unbelief.

Go Deeper

The writer of Hebrews used the idea of a house in discussing the relationship Moses and Jesus have with their followers. This kind of picture is paralleled in other places in the New Testament. Paul told the Ephesians, "So then you are no longer strangers and aliens, but you are fellow citizens with the saints and members of the household of God, built on the foundation of the apostles and prophets, Christ Jesus himself being the cornerstone, in whom the whole structure, being joined together, grows into a holy temple in the Lord. In him you also are being built together into a dwelling place for God by the Spirit" (Eph. 2:19–22). In 1 Corinthians the same idea is applied to the lives of individual believers: "For we are God's fellow workers. You are God's field, God's building. According to the grace of God given to me, like a skilled master builder I laid a foundation, and someone else is building upon it. Let each one take care how he builds upon it. For no one can lay a foundation other than that which is laid, which is Jesus Christ" (1 Cor. 3:9–11).

Through Moses, God gave us the standard called the Law. It sets out God's basic requirements for the human part of His creation. It is not a standard that we can meet on our own. Through Christ, God fulfilled the requirements of the Law on our behalf. God did for us what we could never do for ourselves. And no one else but God could have done that. As God, Jesus met His own standard, and we get the everlasting benefits—if we don't harden our hearts against His gift of salvation.

The focus on the superiority of Jesus in the Letter to the Hebrews doesn't serve to ridicule or downplay the role of others God has included in various stages of His plans. In fact, being mentioned in a group of which Jesus is the superior elevates the entire group to a special category. The prophets and angels already mentioned in the letter were God's messengers. The human messengers wrote much of God's Word; the angelic messengers stepped into history at crucial times. They had significant roles, but none of them can or could replace the central and superior role of Jesus.

Among the Hebrew people, Moses had a special place of honor. Israel became a people as descendants of Abraham, but they became a nation under the leadership of Moses. God used Moses in building the house of Israel. But the writer of Hebrews tells us that Jesus was the builder of the house. In a sense, Moses represented the best of the house itself while Jesus is the one who designed and constructed the house. In modern terms, Moses was an important subcontractor, but Jesus designed, built, and owns the house. Their connected roles are described in this chapter: "Now Moses was faithful in all God's house as a servant, to testify to the things that were to be spoken later, but Christ is faithful over God's house as a son. And we are his house if indeed we hold fast our confidence and our boasting in our hope" (Heb. 3:5–6).

The writer of the Hebrews is not at all afraid to compare the greatest leader in the history of Israel to Jesus because He knows the superiority of the Son of God. Moses was the renowned lawgiver of the Old Testament. But Jesus is superior to him in that Jesus is the great grace-giver of the New Testament. What Moses and the Law couldn't do—bring salvation—Jesus and God's grace did. Grace is superior to the Law partly because Jesus is superior to Moses and all humans.

In Matthew 17:1–13 we read an account of Jesus' Transfiguration. He took three of His disciples up on a mountain, and they were allowed to see Him conversing with two Old Testament figures—Elijah and Moses. The disciples were certainly impressed! Peter's instinctive response was to build a shrine that would highlight these three figures, Jesus, Elijah, and Moses. His plan would display them as equals. At this point, a voice was heard from heaven, saying, "This is my beloved Son, with whom I am well pleased; listen to him" (Matt. 17:5). God Himself made it clear that Elijah and Moses could be in Jesus' company, but no one should forget who was superior.

If we look at the opening statement of Hebrews 3, we face an important challenge we don't dare overlook: "Consider Jesus" (v. 1). In other words, isn't it about time we begin to fix our minds on someone worthy of our thoughts and to take out of our minds all the politicians, all the Hollywood stars, and all the sports figures? Perhaps more than at any time in history, we are guilty of choosing celebrity status over substance. We honor the opinions of people whose only claim to authority is that they have appeared in several movies or read the news on a tele-prompter. The invitation in the

"When the world and our own pursuits minimize and ignore Jesus, we are acting with hardened hearts. No wonder our lives are so unsettled. No wonder we can't 'enter His rest' and find a sense of purpose in life."

letter to the Hebrews is to consider Jesus seriously, perhaps for the first time. And when we think about Jesus, we must always think of Him in terms of His superiority to everyone else. It is not just a bias that Christians have, that the leader of their religion is somehow superior to the leader of other religions. We are not even talking about religion. We are talking about greatness on a scale no one else can match.

A significant part of this chapter is also a warning to us. Not only are Moses and Jesus compared, but also compared are the people who followed Moses and the audience of the letter. The writer warns us not to "harden [our] hearts as in the rebellion" (vv. 8, 15). If the people who followed the great leader Moses rebelled and were punished, how much greater the danger for those who hear about Jesus and turn away? What does it mean to "harden your hearts"? Verses 12–13 explain that hardening of the heart happens when an unbelieving heart (v. 12) is taken in by the deceitfulness of sin (v. 13). When the world and our own pursuits minimize and ignore Jesus, we are acting with hardened hearts. No wonder our lives are so unsettled. No wonder we can't "enter His rest" and find a sense of purpose in life.

What a helpful spiritual prescription we find in verse 1! Every time life gets confusing and we feel like we've lost our way: "Consider Jesus."

Express It

In what ways is your faith under fire today? How is your world hostile? Perhaps the pressure to compromise is internal rather than external. Or perhaps you can't think of any stresses or challenges that are confronting you at the moment. Talk to God about your willingness to trust Him when the going gets tough as well as when the way seems easy. Things can quickly change.

Consider It

As you read Hebrews 3:1–19, consider these questions:

1) In what ways are Jesus and Moses alike? How are they different?

_____

_____

_____

2) How does this chapter explain why Jesus deserves more honor than Moses?

_____

_____

_____

3) What does this chapter say about us as the household of God?

_____

_____

_____

4) What should be the limits when we look at others as examples or models to pattern our spiritual lives after?

_____

_____

_____

5) How have other believers pointed you to Christ by their examples?

_____

_____

_____

6) Where in your life do you have to pay special attention to God's Word because of your tendency to harden your heart and will against His guidance?

_____

_____

_____

7) How many different kinds of "rest" can you list that are prevented when we are in rebellion against God?

_____

_____

_____

Lesson 4

The Greatest High Priest

God has raised up great leaders for His people throughout history. But none of them has been able to accomplish what Jesus alone accomplished. He brought people real rest. He brought people into peace with God.

Hebrews 4:1–16

4 Therefore, while the promise of entering his rest still stands, let us fear lest any of you should seem to have failed to reach it. ²For good news came to us just as to them, but the message they heard did not benefit them, because they were not united by faith with those who listened. ³For we who have believed enter that rest, as he has said,

> "As I swore in my wrath,
> 'They shall not enter my rest,'"

although his works were finished from the foundation of the world. ⁴For he has somewhere spoken of the seventh day in this way: "And God rested on the seventh day from all his works." ⁵And again in this passage he said,

> "They shall not enter my rest."

⁶Since therefore it remains for some to enter it, and those who formerly received the good news failed to enter because of disobedience, ⁷again he appoints a certain day, "Today," saying through David so long afterward, in the words already quoted,

> "Today, if you hear his voice,
> do not harden your hearts."

⁸For if Joshua had given them rest, God would not have spoken of another day later on. ⁹So then, there remains a Sabbath rest for the people of God, ¹⁰for whoever has entered God's rest has also rested from his works as God did from his.

¹¹Let us therefore strive to enter that rest, so that no one may fall by the same sort of disobedience. ¹²For the word of God is living and active, sharper than any two-edged sword, piercing to the division of soul and of spirit, of joints and of marrow, and discerning the thoughts and intentions of the heart. ¹³And no creature is hidden from his sight, but all are naked and exposed to the eyes of him to whom we must give account.

Key Verse

For the word of God is living and active, sharper than any two-edged sword, piercing to the division of soul and of spirit, of joints and of marrow, and discerning the thoughts and intentions of the heart (Heb. 4:12).

Jesus the Great High Priest

¹⁴Since then we have a great high priest who has passed through the heavens, Jesus, the Son of God, let us hold fast our confession. ¹⁵For we do not have a high priest who is unable to sympathize with our weaknesses, but one who in every respect has been tempted as we are, yet without sin. ¹⁶Let us then with confidence draw near to the throne of grace, that we may receive mercy and find grace to help in time of need.

Go Deeper

The Bible uses a number of pictures to describe itself. Hebrews 4:12 contains one of the most powerful ideas about the effectiveness of God's Word in a person's life. Based on Ephesians 6:17, we often call the Bible "the sword of the Spirit" as part of the spiritual armor with which God equips the believer. As a sword, God's Word is a weapon in spiritual warfare. But the passage in Hebrews 4 highlights a different purpose of God's Word. It doesn't call the Bible a sword but rather something "sharper" than a sword. The context shifts from the sword of the Spirit as a weapon in external conflict to a tool God uses in His internal work in our lives.

God's Word deals with the deepest parts of what it means to be human. It takes into account matters of the "joints and marrow" (the physical body) and reveals truth about the soul, the spirit, and the heart of a person. God's Word understands—discerns—us more deeply than we can know ourselves. God's Word represents "his sight" (Heb. 4:13) into our lives, from which nothing is hidden.

To apply another of the Bible's pictures of itself, we can approach God's Word as a faithful and true mirror (James 1:22–25) in which we can see who we are and what we should do. We will never see ourselves more clearly than by means of the pictures we find in God's Word.

The step is very small between comparing Jesus and Moses in chapter 3 and comparing Jesus' priestly work and the work of the priestly system in Israel in chapter 4. After all, the first high priest was Moses' brother, Aaron. Chapter 4 introduces Jesus as high priest, and Hebrews will enlarge on that description in the chapters to come. Most of this chapter, however, focuses on the meaning of "God's rest" and how we can share in it. The central importance of "rest" leads directly to Jesus' role in God's plan. In a sense, the writer of Hebrews describes one of the effective areas of Jesus' ministry before he introduces the particular title Jesus earned in His work for us—High Priest.

Chapter 4 continues an argument that began in chapter 3 with the failure of the people Moses led to "enter his rest" (v. 1). Whatever "rest" is, we can say it is a promise of God, and that promise was not nullified by the people who died in the wilderness or fulfilled by Israel's eventual entry into the Promised Land. Later in the chapter we are told, "For if Joshua had given them rest, God would not have spoken of

> **"** *God's Word deals with the deepest parts of what it means to be human. God's Word understands—discerns—us more deeply than we can know ourselves. God's Word represents 'his sight' (v. 13) into our lives, from which nothing is hidden.* **"**

another day later on" (v. 8). A deeper, broader, and eternal promise is the subject of these verses.

The idea of "rest" that we find in Hebrews is based on two significant Old Testament passages:

> And on the seventh day God finished his work that he had done, and he rested on the seventh day from all his work that he had done. (Gen. 2:2)

> Therefore I swore in my wrath, "They shall not enter my rest." (Ps. 95:11 and the verses that precede it)

The promise of rest still stands for those who are willing to turn from rebellion and disobedience. According to this chapter, "There remains a Sabbath rest for the people of God, for whoever has entered God's rest has also rested from his works as God did from his" (Heb. 4:9–10). Notice the progression of invitation that begins with verse 11. We are to be diligent to enter God's rest by accepting Christ as our Savior (v. 11), based on the revelation of God's Word (v. 12), since we have a high priest, Jesus (v. 14), who has made certain that we can "draw near to the throne of grace" (v. 16). Where is God? He sits on His throne. That's where He rests, dwells, remains. The rest that we seek is offered to us in Christ through a combination of mercy and grace (v. 16). We can be sure that if we "receive mercy" (v. 16) from God and "find grace" (v. 16) in Him, we have also found rest. One of Jesus' powerful descriptions of what He came to offer us is found in Matthew 11:28–30:

Come to me, all who labor and are heavy laden, and I will give you rest. Take my yoke upon you, and learn from me, for I am gentle and lowly in heart, and you will find rest for your souls. For my yoke is easy, and my burden is light." (Matt. 11:28–30)

The writer of Hebrews makes sure that we don't mistake the idea of "rest" with effortlessness or lethargy. He says, "Let us therefore strive to enter that rest, so that no one may fall by the same sort of disobedience" (Heb. 4:11). Couple this with phrases such as "let us fear" (v. 1) and "let us hold fast to our confession" (v. 14), and a picture of alertness and willingness develops. *Rest,* as Hebrews use the word, is a synonym for *salvation.* This is indicated by describing the message that leads to rest in verses 5–6 as "the good news." And the desired response is the same: "For we who have believed enter that rest" (v. 3).

This chapter records three wonderful gifts that God, makes available to us: the message of rest, the Word of God, and Jesus, the superior high priest. The message reminds us that there is still room for us in God's rest. The Word of God, a spiritual two-edged scalpel, constantly "operates" on our lives to bring healing. And our superior high priest sympathizes with our weaknesses and has done something about them.

So how do we rise to the challenge of this chapter? How do we "hold fast to our confession"? We do so by continually acting on what we see in the last verse: "Let us then with confidence draw near to the throne of grace, that we may receive mercy and find grace to help in time of need" (v. 16). Both the source of what we need and the strength to hold on we find in Jesus, who will later in Hebrews be described as "the founder and perfecter of our faith" (12:2).

Express It

One of the classic old hymns of the faith is "Solid Rock," based in part on Matthew 7:24–27. It also speaks about resting in a way that echoes this chapter from Hebrews. The second stanza begins, When darkness veils His lovely face, I rest on His unchanging grace. Talk to God about your trust in Him that gives rest now and hope for eternal rest later.

Consider It

As you read Hebrews 4:1–16, consider these questions:

1) In what way does the writer point to the importance of the word *today*?

_____

_____

_____

2) How do you think of salvation as rest?

_____

_____

_____

3) How does the writer compare the response of those who have heard the Gospel in the past to the danger facing those who hear it now?

_____

_____

_____

4) What is the meaning of "Sabbath rest" in the context of this chapter? (See v. 9.)

_____

_____

_____

5) How do these verses describe the power of God's Word? (See vv. 12–13.)

_____

_____

_____

6) What does it mean to you to "with confidence draw near to the throne of grace"? (See v. 16.)

_____

_____

_____

7) Why is it significant that Jesus can do more than sympathize with our weaknesses? (See v. 15.)

_____

_____

_____

The Unique High Priest

Aaron was the first CEP (chief executive priest) in Israel. The directions for religious life were given by God through Moses, but Aaron was appointed to carry them out. God was accomplishing through Aaron a part of what Jesus would eventually do fully and perfectly.

Hebrews 5:1–14

The Handwriting on the Wall

5 For every high priest chosen from among men is appointed to act on behalf of men in relation to God, to offer gifts and sacrifices for sins. ²He can deal gently with the ignorant and wayward, since he himself is beset with weakness. ³Because of this he is obligated to offer sacrifice for his own sins just as he does for those of the people. ⁴And no one takes this honor for himself, but only when called by God, just as Aaron was.

⁵So also Christ did not exalt himself to be made a high priest, but was appointed by him who said to him,

"You are my Son,
today I have begotten you";

⁶as he says also in another place,

"You are a priest forever,
after the order of
Melchizedek."

⁷In the days of his flesh, Jesus offered up prayers and supplications, with loud cries and tears, to him who was able to save him from death, and he was heard because of his reverence. ⁸Although he was a son, he learned obedience through what he suffered. ⁹And being made

---

Key Verse

And being made perfect, he became the source of eternal salvation to all who obey him (Heb. 5:9).

---

perfect, he became the source of eternal salvation to all who obey him, ¹⁰being designated by God a high priest after the order of Melchizedek.

Warning Against Apostasy

¹¹About this we have much to say, and it is hard to explain, since you have become dull of hearing. ¹²For though by this time you ought to be teachers, you need someone to teach you again the basic principles of the oracles of God. You need milk, not solid food, ¹³for everyone who lives on milk is unskilled in the word of righteousness, since he is a child. ¹⁴But solid food is for the mature, for those who have their powers of discernment trained by constant practice to distinguish good from evil.

Go Deeper

Hebrews 5:11–14 introduces a break in the sequence of teaching in this letter. The writer had just made a crucial point, and he wanted to shift the spotlight of response back to the reader. His description of his readers as "dull of hearing" (v. 11) tells us that he expected them to resist or ignore the point he had made about Jesus. The theme of inattention echoes throughout the New Testament. The explanation given for Jesus' use of parables in His teaching has to do with the tendency to be dull of hearing (see Matt. 13:10–17). The objective of spiritual maturity despite the tendency to settle for milk is also a concern of the New Testament. (See 1 Cor. 14:20; Eph. 4:13–14; James 1:2–8.)

(continued)

Go Deeper Continued . . .

The idea of a high priest would have been very familiar to the original audience of this letter. But the writer of Hebrews intended to use the familiar to teach the deeper truth that it was originally designed to represent. Like the Law of Moses, the Aaronic priesthood was a means to God's ends, not the end itself. Both the Law and the priesthood were intended to prepare the world for Christ. The Gospel requires childlike faith from us but pushes us into adult living and loving. We start with "milk," but are not encouraged to make that our diet. The command to love God with all our heart, soul, mind, and strength (see Matt. 22;37) sounds like an adult kind of challenge.

In Hebrews, both chapters 3 and 4 mention Jesus' special identity as our unique High Priest. For the original Jewish readers, the history of the High Priest was closely tied to the giving of the Law during the Exodus. Moses was called to lead the people, and his older brother, Aaron, was appointed as the first high priest. The lineage of the high priest was usually traced back to Aaron and the priestly Levite clan in Israel. But there was a significant and almost mysterious parallel tradition dating back to the time of Abraham. Jesus was from the tribe of Judah and the royal lineage, so His title as priest had to have a different source and, as Hebrews tells us, a different, superior purpose.

The comparison between Aaron and Jesus begins in chapter 4: "Since then we have a great high priest who has passed through the heavens, Jesus, the Son of God, let us hold fast our confession" (v. 14). If we compare Jesus to the great religious leaders of history, we certainly have to compare Him to Aaron, because Aaron was the original great high priest of Israel. In the verse above Jesus is also called a great high priest, and a difference is noted between Christ and Aaron in that Jesus is the one who has "passed through the heavens" while Aaron is the one who has gone through the wilderness.

As we are reminded in chapter 5 of Hebrews, every high priest was "chosen from among men" and is "appointed to act on behalf of men in relation to God, to offer gifts and sacrifices for sins" (v. 1). As a fellow human being "beset with weakness" (v. 2), the high priest could identify with the people he was called to serve. When he presented sacrifices, they were intended to cover his own as well as the people's

"The message of all religious systems [except Christianity] has to do with following a path that promises we can make it by our works. Christianity differs at the source. Christianity is not a religion but a relationship. Jesus promises to be our way because we can't make it on our own."

sins. This was not a chosen career path but a role to which one was called by God (v. 4).

As we have already discovered in Hebrews, Jesus' relationship to God as Son sets Him apart from the angels. His relationship to God sets Him apart from the prophets. And now we learn His relationship to God sets Him apart from all the high priests that ever lived. He never had to sacrifice for His own sins because despite all He went through, He had no sin. (See 4:15.)

But more than Jesus' sonship, He was also born into a special priesthood: "As He says also in another place, 'You are a priest forever after the order of Melchizedek'" (5:6; we'll see more about Melchizedek in chapter 7). The order to which Jesus belongs as a high priest is different from the order in which Aaron belonged. It's not just different—it's better; it's superior.

Everything about Jesus is superior each time we compare Him honestly to anyone else. Hebrews goes on to say, "In the days of his flesh, Jesus offered up prayers and supplications, with loud cries and tears, to him who was able to save him from death, and he was heard because of his reverence" (5:7). Jesus' "loud cries and tears" give us an intimate glimpse of the Lord's devotional life and a reminder of the intense suffering of the cross. There's no one more tender than someone who sympathizes with us to the extent that he could shed a tear with us.

So, how did Jesus become the Superior Savior? How does He stand out among those who have been judged as *religious leaders* throughout history? This chapter of Hebrews offers us part of the answer. Instead of the limited modeling and representing role of the high priest, Jesus was the perfect High Priest. Unlike all the other high priests, He did not have to offer sacrifices for His own sins because He did not sin. Instead of offering sacrifices, He was the sacrifice! Instead of identifying a perfect animal whose blood could represent the settling of a moral debt, Jesus allowed Himself to be that perfect sacrifice.

When we compare Jesus with other religious figures like Buddha or Muhammad, we find all of them made some kind of impression with their lives. But, ultimately, the message of all religious systems has to do with following a path that promises we can make it by our works. Those who follow anyone but Jesus are trying to earn or deserve their rewards. Christianity differs at the source. As has been so often pointed out, Christianity is not a religion but a relationship. Jesus promises to be our way because we can't make it on our own. We need a high priest who can sympathize with us at the human level without joining us at the sin level. Jesus stated this in His eloquent summary of His role in God's plan: "Jesus said to him, 'I am the way, and the truth, and the life. No one comes to the Father except through me'" (John 14:6). When it comes to saviors, Jesus is in a category by Himself.

Express It

As you pray, consider what it means that Jesus understands you deeply. He doesn't have to guess about your feelings, responses, hurts, and anger. He knows these by experience. He can sympathize. And when you realize that you've sinned, He can also forgive. The sinless One is willing to forgive us and cleanse us from all unrighteousness (see 1 John 1:9). When we acknowledge Jesus' understanding and confess our sins, we are treating Him as our High Priest.

Consider It

As you read Hebrews 5:1–14, consider these questions:

1) What is the primary duty of the high priest?

_____

_____

_____

2) In what sense does the high priest do double duty?

_____

_____

_____

3) What feature does Jesus have in common with Melchizedek in this chapter?

_____

_____

_____

4) If this chapter were your introduction to Jesus Christ, what could you say about Him?

_____

_____

_____

5) How does this chapter explain the reasons for Christ's suffering in God's plan?

_____

_____

_____

6) Besides providing us with a perfect model, what else does Jesus offer us?

_____

_____

_____

7) Based on the last 5 verses in this chapter, how would you describe your present spiritual diet?

_____

_____

_____

Strive for Spiritual Maturity

While we're in our mother's womb, our objective is to be born. But once we are born, we have a whole new goal—to grow up. We can't grow up until we are born, but once we're born, we can't stay infants. That's not how God designed our physical lives. And it's not how He designed our spiritual lives either.

Hebrews 6:1–20

6 Therefore let us leave the elementary doctrine of Christ and go on to maturity, not laying again a foundation of repentance from dead works and of faith toward God, ²and of instruction about washings, the laying on of hands, the resurrection of the dead, and eternal judgment. ³And this we will do if God permits. ⁴For it is impossible, in the case of those who have once been enlightened, who have tasted the heavenly gift, and have shared in the Holy Spirit, ⁵and have tasted the goodness of the word of God and the powers of the age to come, ⁶and then have fallen away, to restore them again to repentance, since they are crucifying once again the Son of God to their own harm and holding him up to contempt. ⁷For land that has drunk the rain that often falls on it, and produces a crop useful to those for whose sake it is cultivated, receives a blessing from God. ⁸But if it bears thorns and thistles, it is worthless and near to being cursed, and its end is to be burned.

⁹Though we speak in this way, yet in your case, beloved, we feel sure of better things—things that belong to salvation. ¹⁰For God is not unjust so as to overlook your work and the love that you have shown for his name in serving the saints, as you still do. ¹¹And we desire each one of you to show the same earnestness to have the full assurance of hope until the end, ¹²so that you may not be sluggish, but imitators of those who through faith and patience inherit the promises.

Key Verse

Though we speak in this way, yet in your case, beloved, we feel sure of better things—things that belong to salvation (Heb. 6:9).

¹³For when God made a promise to Abraham, since he had no one greater by whom to swear, he swore by himself, ¹⁴saying, "Surely I will bless you and multiply you." ¹⁵And thus Abraham, having patiently waited, obtained the promise. ¹⁶For people swear by something greater than themselves, and in all their disputes an oath is final for confirmation. ¹⁷So when God desired to show more convincingly to the heirs of the promise the unchangeable character of his purpose, he guaranteed it with an oath, ¹⁸so that by two unchangeable things, in which it is impossible for God to lie, we who have fled for refuge might have strong encouragement to hold fast to the hope set before us. ¹⁹We have this as a sure and steadfast anchor of the soul, a hope that enters into the inner place behind the curtain, ²⁰where Jesus has gone as a forerunner on our behalf, having become a high priest forever after the order of Melchizedek.

Go Deeper

There are many people who believe the Bible is God's Word but know very little about what's in it. Many of them may have "tasted the goodness of the word of God" (Heb. 6:5) but have moved on to other supposed spiritual food—perhaps to their eternal loss. There are many who "listen to the Word" but never get around to "doing the Word" (see James 1:22–27). Ultimately, it's not what we say we believe about the Bible that matters but what the Bible does in our lives. We can't continue to settle for spiritual milk (Heb. 5:12) just because that's where we started. If that's all we consume, we are left "unskilled in the word of righteousness" (5:13) and have not developed "discernment" (5:14).

We need to experience the scalpel-like effectiveness of God's Word continually in our daily lives (see Heb. 4:12–13). We need to move beyond the correct position on biblical inspiration until we are experiencing fully the four objectives God intended to accomplish by His Word: "All Scripture is breathed out by God and profitable for *teaching,* for *reproof,* for *correction,* and for *training* in *righteousness,* that the man of God may be competent, equipped for every good work" (2 Tim. 3:16–17, italics added). God's purpose is to grow us up into Christlike people who live righteously— the way He wants us to live.

Foundations are essential parts of buildings. Foundations determine whether a structure will stand. But foundations are not living spaces and working spaces; they make those things possible and lasting. Hebrews 6 opens with an ongoing appeal to the reader not only to have the right foundation (Christ) but to persist in building an authentic life on that foundation. This closely parallels the apostle Paul's lesson to the Corinthians: "According to the grace of God given to me, like a skilled master builder I laid a foundation, and someone else is building upon it. Let each one take care how he builds upon it. For no one can lay a foundation other than that which is laid, which is Jesus Christ" (1 Cor. 3:10–11). When the writer of Hebrews says, "let us leave" (Heb. 6:1), he is not speaking about moving to build somewhere else but building a life-structure on the foundation we already have (Christ) that is worthy of God.

The question that almost always comes up when people read Hebrews 6:4–8 has to do with the certainty of salvation. Is the writer saying that someone can come to genuine faith in Christ, experience salvation, and then lose his or her citizenship in God's kingdom?

"We need to remember why we came to Christ in the first place, but we can't just 'live' there. That's the foundation. And the One who is our foundation wants us to build something useful and beautiful on Him."

How much does "tasting" and "sharing" (vv. 4–5) have to do with the process of moving a soul from eternity in hell to eternity in heaven? Is it possible to taste and share but never exercise saving faith?

First, these questions are not central to the writer's purpose here. As he states in verse 9, he is not accusing his readers of being in the category of "once found, now lost again." He does not address them directly but is speaking of others whom his readers probably know, who have come very close to the kingdom but never entered. They have experienced and even exhibited many of the marks of the saving process (repentance, enlightenment) but have turned away. These are people who know everything they need to know in order to truly believe, and yet they fall away in ongoing unbelief. In the excruciating words of this chapter, these are people who have realized that Christ was crucified for them but have not accepted that fact. The author's point is that if they were found and then lost again, it would necessitate Christ being crucified again to win them back, and God will not permit that to happen.

Second, the writer's intent in even mentioning those who have not been born into the kingdom of God is to make the point that when we are not diligent and persistent in spiritual growth, we are open to others' wondering about the genuineness of our spiritual lives. If we quack like a duck, walk like a duck, and live like a duck, why should the other ducks believe us when we claim to be new creatures in Christ? It is almost a rule in ministry that those people who are struggling with the certainty of their faith are usually people who have been lax in spiritual growth. They may slide into doubts, but before that happens, their lives typically exhibit low interest and little commitment to spiritual growth and health.

It's not surprising that this chapter immediately turns to the subject of certainty. God's promises are certain. What He says He will do, He will do. The Christian life is not a continual round of second-guessing the depth of our faith but a continual process in which God works in us to bring about His purposes. The writer of Hebrews would shout "Amen" to Paul's words: "And I am sure of this, that he who began a good work in you will bring it to completion at the day of Jesus Christ" (Phil. 1:6). That expresses the desires that motivated the writing of the letter to the Hebrews in the first place. Hebrews 6:10–12 touches on the evidences in the lives of the audience that their faith is genuine. That faith needs to be stirred up because it is in danger of being "sluggish" (v. 12). We can put ourselves somewhere on the continuum pictured in this chapter: we tend to be either uncertain of our faith because we are not growing or sluggish in our faith because we have become spiritually lazy. It's time for us to become "imitators of those who through faith and patience inherit the promises" (v. 12).

Just before returning to the subject of Jesus' Melchizedek-style priesthood, the writer of Hebrews penned some unforgettable words of support: God's certain promises make it possible that "we who have fled for refuge might have strong encouragement to hold fast to the hope set before us" (v. 18). We need to remember why we came to Christ in the first place, but we can't just "live" there. That's the foundation. And the One who is our foundation wants us to build something useful and beautiful on Him.

Express It

Take verse 7 of this chapter and make it into a prayer. See yourself as a field waiting for God's rain and the blessing of God's promises. They are certain (see vv. 13–18). Ask God what crops He wants to produce in you and make it your purpose to be that kind of productive field.

Consider It

As you read Hebrews 6:1–20, consider these questions:

1) What fits into the category of "elementary doctrine" (called "milk" in Heb. 5:12)? Why?

_____

_____

2) How is it a hindrance to your spiritual maturity to keep going over and over "elementary doctrine" instead of building on it and going deeper in your understanding?

_____

_____

3) How do we know we are making progress in spiritual growth?

_____

_____

4) Which ones of God's unchanging promises do you rely on the most?

_____

_____

5) What have been the primary evidences of spiritual growth in your life over the last six months?

_____

_____

6) This chapter mentions one thing God can't do. What is it and why is it important?

_____

_____

7) In what different ways does this chapter motivate you to spiritual growth?

_____

_____

The Superior Covenant

The nation of Israel has also been known since ancient times as the people of the covenant. We learn in this lesson that God's original covenant with Israel was based on a deeper, wider, and longer covenant God planned for the world.

Hebrews 7:1–28

The Priestly Order of Melchizedek

7 For this Melchizedek, king of Salem, priest of the Most High God, met Abraham returning from the slaughter of the kings and blessed him, ²and to him Abraham apportioned a tenth part of everything. He is first, by translation of his name, king of righteousness, and then he is also king of Salem, that is, king of peace. ³He is without father or mother or genealogy, having neither beginning of days nor end of life, but resembling the Son of God he continues a priest forever.

⁴See how great this man was to whom Abraham the patriarch gave a tenth of the spoils! ⁵And those descendants of Levi who receive the priestly office have a commandment in the law to take tithes from the people, that is, from their brothers, though these also are descended from Abraham. ⁶But this man who does not have his descent from them received tithes from Abraham and blessed him who had the promises. ⁷It is beyond dispute that the inferior is blessed by the superior. ⁸In the one case tithes are received by mortal men, but in the other case, by one of whom it is testified that he lives. ⁹One might even say that Levi himself, who receives tithes, paid tithes through Abraham, ¹⁰for he was still in the loins of his ancestor when Melchizedek met him.

Jesus Compared to Melchizedek

¹¹Now if perfection had been attainable through the Levitical priesthood (for under it the people received the law), what further need would there have been for another priest to arise after the order of Melchizedek, rather than one named after the order of Aaron? ¹²For when there is a change in the priesthood, there is necessarily a change in the law as well. ¹³For the one of whom these things are spoken belonged to another tribe, from

Key Verse

This makes Jesus the guarantor of a better covenant (Heb. 7:22).

which no one has ever served at the altar. ¹⁴For it is evident that our Lord was descended from Judah, and in connection with that tribe Moses said nothing about priests.

¹⁵This becomes even more evident when another priest arises in the likeness of Melchizedek, ¹⁶who has become a priest, not on the basis of a legal requirement concerning bodily descent, but by the power of an indestructible life. ¹⁷For it is witnessed of him,

"You are a priest forever,
after the order of
Melchizedek."

¹⁸For on the one hand, a former commandment is set aside because of its weakness and uselessness ¹⁹(for the law made nothing perfect); but on the other hand, a better hope is introduced, through which we draw near to God.

²⁰And it was not without an oath. For those who formerly became priests were made such without an oath, ²¹but this one was made a priest with an oath by the one who said to him:

"The Lord has sworn
and will not change his mind,
'You are a priest forever.'"

²²This makes Jesus the guarantor of a better covenant.

²³The former priests were many in number, because they were prevented by death from continuing in office, ²⁴but

he holds his priesthood permanently, because he continues forever. ²⁵Consequently, he is able to save to the uttermost those who draw near to God through him, since he always lives to make intercession for them.

²⁶For it was indeed fitting that we should have such a high priest, holy, innocent, unstained, separated from sinners, and exalted above the heavens. ²⁷He has no need, like those high priests, to offer sacrifices daily, first for his own sins and then for those of the people, since he did this once for all when he offered up himself. ²⁸For the law appoints men in their weakness as high priests, but the word of the oath, which came later than the law, appoints a Son who has been made perfect forever.

Go Deeper

Genesis 14 introduces us to the historical priest-king Melchizedek. He is also mentioned in Psalm 110, a prophetic passage in the Old Testament. These ancient references form the basis for the writer of Hebrews as he explains the connection between God's old covenant and the New Covenant in Christ. This is one of those instances that highlight the importance of knowing the Old Testament in order to understand the New Testament.

Hebrews 7:1–10 reviews the history of Abraham's honor of Melchizedek by giving him a tithe of the spoils of battle (see Gen. 14:5–20). These verses explain the uniqueness of Melchizedek's name and his role as priest-king in what later became the city of David, Jerusalem. Melchizedek was a priest of El Elyon, God Most High.

We don't know anything about Melchizedek's ancestry: without father, without mother (see Heb. 7:3). He became a ready-made figure of speech to show us the Lord Jesus and a priesthood superior to the one that came from Abraham's loins (v. 10). That's how Psalm 110 mentions the one David calls Lord. This idea takes another step forward in a crucial moment in Jesus' life, just days before His death. Matthew 22:41–46 records the turning point in Jesus' ministry between responding to the attempts of others to make Him betray Himself and His final steps toward the cross. He used Psalm 110:1 to pose a question about David's dual use of the word Lord. Jesus pointed out the curious fact that David called someone Lord who was also his descendant (son). His opponents had no answer, or were unwilling to acknowledge what we know—Jesus was that answer.

The night before His crucifixion, Jesus took the cup and said, "This is my blood of the covenant, which is poured out for many for the forgiveness of sins" (Matt. 26:28). Jesus was telling His disciples, though they didn't realize it until a little later, that His blood completed or fulfilled the original covenant God established with Israel. The lessons about God's willingness to forgive—acted out in the sacrifice of millions of perfect lambs—were about to be realized in the death of Jesus, the perfect Lamb of God. God's covenant with man was about to get better. Hebrews 7 shows us at least three ways in which the New Covenant ratified with Jesus' blood was an improvement on the Old Covenant.

Today we don't deal so much with covenants; we deal with contracts. There is a significant difference between the two. A contract represents a legal agreement, and it is broken when either or both of the two parties fails to keep its promises. A covenant is more like the ties between a husband and wife or even between a parent and child. Contracts usually have a time limit; covenants are intended to be lasting. Unfortunately, we often treat marriage like a contract today, but God's intention in the design of marriage was that it be a life-long covenant between a man and woman. God often speaks of Israel as His Bride (see Isa. 49:18; 62:5). He also says, "Can a woman forget her nursing child, that she should have no compassion on the son of her womb? Even these may forget, yet I will not forget you" (Isa. 49:15). Now, that's God's covenant with us. He has a heart attachment to us. There's a connection between God and us as individuals. Jesus makes it the perfect covenant.

First, the New Covenant brings better blessings. If we define *blessing* as "speaking or bringing good into a person's life," we conclude that while the Old Covenant brought good into the lives of those who lived faithfully under it, those who are blessed by the New Covenant receive something even better. The writer of Hebrews (Heb. 7:1–10) bases this conclusion on the differences between Abraham's connection with Melchizedek in Genesis 14 and the covenant established with Abraham through Moses. Since Jesus was a priest "after the order of Melchizedek" (Heb. 7:11), He offers us blessings

> *"He gave us through His Son the blessing of a rescue (salvation by grace) when we got lost. A better covenant brings a better blessing. . . . With Jesus, we have a better guarantee of tomorrow."*

by faith. From Abraham's descendant Moses, we receive the blessing of God's revealed standard: His commandments or the Law. Through Christ, we receive the greater blessing of a solution for our failure to keep God's Law. God gave us the blessing of a moral map for living through Moses. Then He gave us through His Son the blessing of a rescue (salvation by grace) when we got lost. A better covenant brings a better blessing.

Second, the New Covenant brings better hope (vv. 11–19). Jesus was of the tribe of Judah, the tribe of royalty, not the priestly tribe of Levi (Aaron). The Old Covenant brought the hope of peace to those who kept it, but through Jesus we have a better covenant and therefore a better hope. The Old Covenant brought an unavoidable awareness of sinfulness under God's perfect standard; the New Covenant brought God's answer for our sinfulness. Under the Old Covenant people hoped based on God's promise; under the New Covenant, the promise has been fulfilled. Our hope is a living hope, one that purifies us. The hope of the Old Testament was adequate; the hope of the New Testament is better.

Third, the New Covenant comes with an eternal guarantee (vv. 20–28). The New Covenant brings a better guarantee because it was sworn with a God-given oath. And the oath is guaranteed by Jesus, the everlasting One. The Old Covenant cannot compare. With Jesus, we have a better guarantee of tomorrow. The role of the priest under the Old Covenant was subject to the lifespan of the priest, but the New Covenant is overseen by the Priest who is Life. As the risen

Son of God, Jesus is not only our perfect High Priest, but He is also our eternal (forever) High Priest.

No wonder, then, that Jesus is called the "guarantor of a better covenant" (v. 22). Notice the words that describe His ongoing work for us: "permanently" (v. 24); "forever" (v. 24); "save to the uttermost" (v. 25); "he always lives" (v. 25). We too can "draw near to God through him" (v. 25) because Jesus is the "Son who has been made perfect forever" (v. 28)—our Superior Savior.

Express It

Go through the devotional above and list all the ways that Jesus provides a better covenant, then write out the verses that support this truth. Each day this week, take one or two of these truths and meditate on what it means to you. In your prayer time, give thanks to the Father for providing a better covenant through our High Priest and His Son, Jesus.

Consider It

As you read Hebrews 7:1–28, consider these questions:

1) What do you learn from Hebrews 7 that helps you understand Genesis 14 better?

_____

_____

_____

2) How do we know that Abraham considered Melchizedek someone with greatness?

_____

_____

_____

3) In what ways is Jesus compared to Melchizedek in this chapter?

_____

_____

_____

4) How, according to this chapter, did Christ become High Priest?

_____

_____

_____

5) What makes Jesus unique as a high priest?

_____

_____

_____

6) How do you respond to Jesus as your High Priest?

_____

_____

_____

7) How does Jesus' role as High Priest affect our approach to God?

_____

_____

_____

Lesson

8

Better Covenant, Better Promises

Good is okay. Better is better. Velveeta cheese is good; Gorgonzola is better. Paris, Maine, is good; Paris, France, is better. In life we often settle for good when God has better things in mind for us.

Hebrews 8 describes the better promises that come with a better covenant.

Hebrews 8:1–13

Jesus, High Priest of a Better Covenant

8 Now the point in what we are saying is this: we have such a high priest, one who is seated at the right hand of the throne of the Majesty in heaven, ²a minister in the holy places, in the true tent that the Lord set up, not man. ³For every high priest is appointed to offer gifts and sacrifices; thus it is necessary for this priest also to have something to offer. ⁴Now if he were on earth, he would not be a priest at all, since there are priests who offer gifts according to the law. ⁵They serve a copy and shadow of the heavenly things. For when Moses was about to erect the tent, he was instructed by God, saying, "See that you make everything according to the pattern that was shown you on the mountain." ⁶But as it is, Christ has obtained a ministry that is as much more excellent than the old as the covenant he mediates is better, since it is enacted on better promises. ⁷For if that first covenant had been faultless, there would have been no occasion to look for a second.

⁸For he finds fault with them when he says:

"Behold, the days are coming,
    declares the Lord,
    when I will establish a new
        covenant with the house
        of Israel
    and with the house of Judah,
⁹not like the covenant that I
        made with their fathers
    on the day when I took them
        by the hand to bring
        them out of the land
        of Egypt.
For they did not continue in my
        covenant,
    and so I showed no concern for
        them, declares the Lord.
¹⁰For this is the covenant that I
        will make with the house
        of Israel

after those days, declares the
        Lord:
I will put my laws into their
        minds,
    and write them on their
        hearts,
and I will be their God,
    and they shall be my people.

¹¹And they shall not teach, each
        one his neighbor
    and each one his brother,
        saying, 'Know the Lord,'
for they shall all know me,
    from the least of them to the
        greatest.
¹²For I will be merciful toward
        their iniquities,
    and I will remember their sins
        no more."

¹³In speaking of a new covenant, he makes the first one obsolete. And what is becoming obsolete and growing old is ready to vanish away.

Key Verse

But as it is, Christ has obtained a ministry that is as much more excellent than the old as the covenant he mediates is better, since it is enacted on better promises (Heb. 8:6).

Go Deeper

If we start in Genesis and read all the way through to the end of Malachi, we are amazed by the constant promises made and kept by God. Let's look at some of the promises God made to people in the Old Testament. One of the most familiar is Psalm 23, an affirmation of various ways in which God demonstrates He is a caring shepherd. David was living his life each day counting on God's present promises and looking forward to the day when he would be "in the house of the Lord, forever" (Ps. 23:6). The psalmist wasn't quite certain what the house of the Lord would look like. He didn't exactly know where it was. He didn't exactly know how large it would be or how it would be configured or who was going to build it. But he understood that God had made him certain promises upon which he could count.

Even in the middle of judgment, God included one of the most precious promises. Genesis 3:15 describes the enmity between the offspring of the serpent and the offspring of Eve in the words, "He shall bruise your head, and you shall bruise his heel." This was the original promise of a savior, and it goes back to the very beginning. The writer of Hebrews includes another of these promises, found in Jeremiah 31:31–34, in Hebrews 7:8–12. Actually, God's promises are being given or fulfilled on almost every page of the Old Testament.

The New Testament (the word *testament* means "covenant") presents the same God of promise that we meet in the Old Testament, but here His promises have a much more definite flavor to them. The New Covenant promises have a permanent tone. For example, Jesus says to Nicodemus, "And as Moses lifted up the serpent in the wilderness, so must the Son of Man be lifted up, that whoever believes in him may have eternal life" (John 3:14–15). God's original promise had been to bring life to those Israelites bitten by poisonous serpents (Num. 21:8–9); His upgraded promise was to bring eternal life to those bitten by sin. For more of this, see John 5:24, John 6:32–35 and John 8:31–32. These are promises with present and eternal outcomes. They are better promises! The promises of the New Covenant are better promises than the promises of the Old Covenant; not that the Old Covenant wasn't good. It was very good. But Christ's promises are better because they are eternal.

In the last lesson we briefly looked at the better blessings, hope, and guarantees that have come to us through Christ's New Covenant. Chapter 8 of Hebrews focuses on the impact of God's promises seen in His Covenant with us.

When we try to understand God's promises, it's important to admit from the outset that the differences between God's promises and our promises are like the differences between lightning and a lightning bug. Like Him, we make promises; unlike Him, we often break ours—even the ones we make to Him. God not only keeps His promises; He often improves on them, doing even more than He promised. Or to put it another way, no matter how hard we try, we can't fully understand all the implications of God's promises. Even His promises drive us back to our need to appreciate, worship, and submit to Him.

Hebrews 8:1 wraps up the lesson from chapter 7 and states the theme of this chapter. "Now the point in what we are saying is this: we have such a high priest" (v. 1). Basically, he writes, "I'm going to sum up now the heart of this letter." He goes on to identify the High Priest, to tell us where He is, and to remind us what He is doing.

We need to remember that our High Priest is not in a tabernacle making His way through the desert. Our High Priest is not in a temple somewhere in Israel. Our High Priest is seated at the right hand of God. Our High Priest is in heaven. God's residence never was in temples built with human hands (see Acts 7:48; Heb. 9:11, 24), but He did visit those places and structures that He declared holy. His presence filled the tabernacle (Ex. 40:34–35) as well as the temple (1 Kings 8:10–11). But because both the tabernacle and temple were temporary, they could not be God's dwelling place—for He "dwells" in eternity. And that's where Christ ministers the New Covenant.

Everything about Jesus and what He brings to you is better. So, the writer of Hebrews says, first of all, that our High Priest is at the right hand of the Father. Now, that's the place of power—at the right hand of the Father. That's the place of privilege—at the right hand of the Father. That's the place of prestige—at the right hand of the Father. And that's the place of proximity—at the right hand of the Father. Jesus is as close to the Father as He can get. With apologies

> *"All the best things in life foreshadow what heaven will be like. As good as life can be, eternal life will be better!"*

to all those who are left-handed, the right hand of God is always the most important place.

The tent in the wilderness (the tabernacle) was good for its time—speaking of God's moving presence. The temple in Jerusalem was good for its time—speaking of God's maintaining presence. But the heavenly "tent" is better for all time—speaking of God's eternal presence.

Consider this question: if you had an opportunity to live in a home built by the best carpenter on the face of the earth or to live in a place that the Lord God of heaven, the perfect, omnipotent, omniscient God created, which would you choose? The choice is a no-brainer. This reminds us of Jesus' words, "'Let not your hearts be troubled. Believe in God; believe also in me. In my Father's house are many rooms. If it were not so, would I have told you that I go to prepare a place for you? And if I go and prepare a place for you, I will come again and will take you to myself, that where I am you may be also'" (John 14:1–3). We can look forward to living in a house built by God!

One of the keys to understanding the message of Hebrews is to remember the relationship between original and copy, object and shadow. That's what this chapter tells us about the Old Covenant tent, the priests, and their sacrifices, "They serve a copy and shadow of the heavenly things. For when Moses was about to erect the tent, he was instructed by God, saying, 'See that you make everything according to the pattern that was shown you on the mountain'" (Heb. 8:5). The plans for the tabernacle and the priesthood were given by God to Moses. And the tabernacle was a scale model, a copy, a shadow, a facsimile of what God already had in heaven. All the best things in life foreshadow what heaven will be like. As good as life can be, eternal life will be better!

God didn't promise us that there would be no disappointment or pain in life. We need to make sure we don't attribute to God promises He didn't make. What's amazing is that despite the sinful condition on earth, God still offers so many wonderful good things. But we can't ever forget that we are meant for a better forever.

The promises of God are great under the Old Covenant. They are better under the New Covenant because there we have exceedingly great and precious promises (see Go Deeper). That's because Jesus provides for us a better covenant, full of promises we will enjoy for eternity.

Express It

Take a few minutes to browse through the Scriptures looking for God's promises. You can start perhaps with the last sentence in Matthew (28:20). Turn these promises over in your mind and apply them to your life. Ask God how He wants you to live based on each of the promises you find. In what ways do God's promises free you to serve Him?

Consider It

As you read Hebrews 8:1–13, consider these questions:

1) What superior aspects of the New Covenant does this chapter point out?

2) Why did God install the New Covenant?

3) How does the New Covenant upgrade the Old one?

4) Why was Jesus not born into a priestly family in Israel?

5) How does God reveal His character in replacing the Old Covenant with the New?

6) How do we know that was His plan all along?

7) To what degree do you think Jeremiah's prophecy (Heb. 8:8–12 and Jer. 31:31–34) has come true for you?

Lesson
9

Better Covenant, Better Sacrifice

When we receive the New Covenant that Jesus established with His blood, we receive a better covenant. It's better because Jesus' work on the cross brings to us a better sacrifice. His sacrifice accomplishes what no other sacrifice could.

Hebrews 9:1–28

The Earthly Holy Place

9 Now even the first covenant had regulations for worship and an earthly place of holiness. ²For a tent was prepared, the first section, in which were the lampstand and the table and the bread of the Presence. It is called the Holy Place. ³Behind the second curtain was a second section called the Most Holy Place, ⁴having the golden altar of incense and the ark of the covenant covered on all sides with gold, in which was a golden urn holding the manna, and Aaron's staff that budded, and the tablets of the covenant. ⁵Above it were the cherubim of glory overshadowing the mercy seat. Of these things we cannot now speak in detail.

⁶These preparations having thus been made, the priests go regularly into the first section, performing their ritual duties, ⁷but into the second only the high priest goes, and he but once a year, and not without taking blood, which he offers for himself and for the unintentional sins of the people. ⁸By this the Holy Spirit indicates that the way into the holy places is not yet opened as long as the first section is still standing ⁹(which is symbolic for the present age). According to this arrangement, gifts and sacrifices are offered that cannot perfect the conscience of the worshiper, ¹⁰but deal only with food and drink and various washings, regulations for the body imposed until the time of reformation.

Redemption Through the Blood of Christ

¹¹But when Christ appeared as a high priest of the good things that have come, then through the greater and more perfect tent (not made with hands, that is, not of this creation) ¹²he entered once for all into the holy places, not by means of the blood of goats and calves but by means of his own blood, thus securing an eternal redemption. ¹³For if the blood of goats and bulls, and the sprinkling

> ## Key Verse
>
> *He entered once for all into the holy places, not by means of the blood of goats and calves but by means of his own blood, thus securing an eternal redemption* (Heb. 9:12).

of defiled persons with the ashes of a heifer, sanctify for the purification of the flesh, ¹⁴how much more will the blood of Christ, who through the eternal Spirit offered himself without blemish to God, purify our conscience from dead works to serve the living God.

¹⁵Therefore he is the mediator of a new covenant, so that those who are called may receive the promised eternal inheritance, since a death has occurred that redeems them from the transgressions committed under the first covenant. ¹⁶For where a will is involved, the death of the one who made it must be established. ¹⁷For a will takes effect only at death, since it is not in force as long as the one who made it is alive. ¹⁸Therefore not even the first covenant was inaugurated without blood. ¹⁹For when every commandment of the law had been declared by Moses to all the people, he took the blood of calves and goats, with water and scarlet wool and hyssop, and sprinkled both the book itself and all the people, ²⁰saying, "This is the blood of the covenant that God commanded for you." ²¹And in the same way he sprinkled with the blood both the tent and all the vessels used in worship. ²²Indeed, under the law almost everything is purified with blood, and without the shedding of blood there is no forgiveness of sins.

[23]Thus it was necessary for the copies of the heavenly things to be purified with these rites, but the heavenly things themselves with better sacrifices than these. [24]For Christ has entered, not into holy places made with hands, which are copies of the true things, but into heaven itself, now to appear in the presence of God on our behalf. [25]Nor was it to offer himself repeatedly, as the high priest enters the holy places every year with blood not his own, [26]for then he would have had to suffer repeatedly since the foundation of the world. But as it is, he has appeared once for all at the end of the ages to put away sin by the sacrifice of himself. [27]And just as it is appointed for man to die once, and after that comes judgment, [28]so Christ, having been offered once to bear the sins of many, will appear a second time, not to deal with sin but to save those who are eagerly waiting for him.

Go Deeper

In Hebrews 9:22 we read, "Indeed, under the law almost everything is purified with blood, and without the shedding of blood there is no forgiveness of sins." Have you ever wondered about that expression, "almost everything is purified with blood"? Did he mean all things or did he actually mean almost all things?

God's Word does not equivocate. When He says almost all things, He means almost all things. If we go back through the Old Testament, we find that there were exceptions to the cleansing of blood. For example, when the Old Testament Israelites went to war, there was plunder after a victory. Numbers 31:21–24 instructed the people to take the silver or gold plunder and pass it through the fire so that all of the dross was burned off. But if the plunder was something like clothing, they were to wash it in water, and that's how it was cleansed (see also Ex. 19:10; Lev. 16:26).

Though there were clearly exceptions to blood purification (generally clothes), there were no spiritual exceptions to this rule. When Scripture says *almost* all things are purified by blood, it is saying that there are some exceptions in the physical world, but there are no exceptions in the spiritual world. Why? The reason is found in the rest of the verse: "Without the shedding of blood there is no forgiveness of sins" (Heb. 9:22).

Now, the word *forgiveness* (also translated *remission*) comes from a word that means "to pay, to release from an obligation." So, the statement is related to the spiritual area in which sins create a debt or obligation that must be settled. But there is only one way such an obligation can be settled: "Without the shedding of blood there is no payment" (v. 22, paraphrase). In other words, "If there is no adequate blood shed on your behalf, there is no payment for your sin."

Hebrews 9:23 explains the situation. Concerning all those countless Old Testament sacrifices God says, "That was just a photocopy, that was just a facsimile—a facsimile of the real thing that's in heaven—the real thing being the blood of Jesus Christ."

Most Jewish people today know that the shedding of blood was necessary for remitting sin. But they see it now as tradition—something they did. But they don't see the necessity of that principle, nor do they see the fact that what their fathers were doing was simply a photocopy of what was real.

And what is real is what Jesus did when He shed His blood for us. What is real is what Jesus has done for all mankind, for all of time.

The first ten verses of Hebrews 9 give us a quick description of the layout of the original tabernacle. Both the Holy Place and the Most Holy Place are mentioned with their furnishings. The writer wanted the readers to have a vivid picture in their minds before launching his next lesson on the superior Savior. But he didn't have space to engage in a detailed explanation of the tabernacle parts, so after listing them he writes, "Of these things we cannot now speak in detail" (v. 5).

With the furniture in place, it's time to focus on a central function of the tabernacle—providing a place to carry out the "regulations for worship" (v. 1). The Holy Place was continually visited by the priests, "performing their ritual duties" (v. 6). But the Most Holy Place received only one visit each year by the high priest who came with sacrificial blood offered for his own sins and the sins of the people (see v. 7). The curtain that separated the two areas indicated "that the way into the holy places is not yet opened as long as the first section is still standing" (v. 8). As long as the Old Covenant rules were in place, access to God's presence was severely restricted. Why? Because the old system had limited effectiveness. It could not "perfect the conscience of the worshiper" (v. 9). It could cover sins but not remove them "until the time of reformation" (v. 10).

Hebrews 9:11–28 contrasts the role of the traditional high priest and his offering of sacrificial blood with the superior role of Jesus, who was both High Priest and sacrifice at the same time. Like succeeding waves breaking on shore, the tide of the argument for Jesus' superiority rises higher and higher. First (vv. 11–12), Jesus entered the "greater and more perfect" tabernacle in heaven, not the stone and marble temple in Jerusalem. He entered the ultimate Most Holy Place "not by means of the blood of goats and calves but by means of his own blood" (v. 12). Because His sacrifice was eternal, Jesus was able to secure "eternal redemption" (v. 12) in contrast to the yearly temporary redemption performed by the high priest.

Second (vv. 13–14), though the death and blood of animals functioned "for the purification of the flesh" (v. 13), Jesus' blood and self-sacrifice work to "purify our conscience from dead works to

> *"We can personalize what Jesus did—He put away my sin by the sacrifice of Himself. Once we have done that, we are no longer waiting for death and judgment. We are waiting for Him."*

serve the living God" (v. 14). The comparison here is similar to the difference between washing our hands and having our hearts and souls cleansed. There may be similarities in the process, but the results are significantly different. Under Jesus' blood, people are set free to live for God!

Third (vv. 15–26), because death confirms a last will and testament while blood confirms a covenant in this world, which is a shadow of reality, we can expect a superior (eternal) action to be taking place in heaven. So the principle "without the shedding of blood there is no forgiveness of sins" (v. 22) gives us the high tide of conviction about our condition. The forgiveness we long for requires death. We can't bargain, buy, or earn forgiveness. It comes through the blood of Another. But along with the hard message comes the word of hope that Christ is able to provide what we need (a sacrificial death). And because of who He is, His death on a single occasion is sufficient to do what countless repeated animal deaths could never accomplish.

Hebrews 9 ends with a powerful personal application that is difficult to miss. The subject shifts from the death of animal sacrifices and the death of Jesus to our deaths—a one-time experience (v. 27). Death is not followed by second chances or a change of mind. Death is followed by judgment. The time to deal with the inevitable judgment is before death, not after. That's why considering Jesus' death and its purpose is so crucial to us. Our eternal destiny hangs in the balance. If we have not allowed Jesus to apply His death to our sin and our lives, then all we have to look forward to is judgment without defense. But Jesus offers us His defense for the judgment. His death served to "put away sin by the sacrifice of himself" (v. 26). We can personalize what Jesus did—He put away *my* sin by the sacrifice of Himself. Once we have done that, we are no longer waiting for death and judgment. We are waiting for Him—"Christ, having been offered once to bear the sins of many, will appear a second time, not to deal with sin but to save those who are eagerly waiting for him" (v. 28).

Express It

We usually don't think twice about walking into the sanctuary in our church along with the rest of the worshipers. We take admission for granted. Curiously, this often changes if we enter the worship space alone. We feel a little more exposed and vulnerable. This is healthy spiritually because it helps us focus attention on why we get to approach God boldly—Someone opened a way for us. Put this into practice sometime in the next few weeks. Enter a place of worship slowly and thoughtfully.

Consider It

As you read Hebrews 9:1–28, consider these questions:

1) In order to enter the earthly Most Holy Place, what three restrictions had to be met?

_____

_____

_____

2) What was the Holy Spirit's point in having a separating curtain between the parts of the tabernacle?

_____

_____

_____

3) Why is the tearing of the curtain in the temple (see Matt. 27:45–54) significant in light of this chapter of Hebrews?

_____

_____

_____

4) What benefits do believers in Christ receive from His sacrifice?

_____

_____

_____

5) How does the writer of Hebrews connect death and blood with the confirmation of a will and a covenant? (See Heb. 9:15–18.)

_____

_____

_____

6) Why is it important and significant that Jesus' sacrifice was "once for all" (v. 12; 7:27)?

_____

_____

_____

7) How have you personalized Jesus' blood sacrifice on your behalf?

_____

_____

_____

Just Live By Faith

If everything we have been studying about the superior character and role of Jesus is true, then our lives should be different from those around us. This chapter lays the groundwork for living a life of faith.

Hebrews 10:1–39

Christ's Sacrifice Once for All

10 For since the law has but a shadow of the good things to come instead of the true form of these realities, it can never, by the same sacrifices that are continually offered every year, make perfect those who draw near. ²Otherwise, would they not have ceased to be offered, since the worshipers, having once been cleansed, would no longer have any consciousness of sins? ³But in these sacrifices there is a reminder of sins every year. ⁴For it is impossible for the blood of bulls and goats to take away sins.

⁵Consequently, when Christ came into the world, he said,

"Sacrifices and offerings you have
        not desired,
    but a body have you prepared
        for me;
⁶in burnt offerings and sin
        offerings
    you have taken no pleasure.
⁷Then I said, 'Behold, I have
        come to do your will,
        O God,
    as it is written of me in the
        scroll of the book.'"

⁸When he said above, "You have neither desired nor taken pleasure in sacrifices and offerings and burnt offerings and sin offerings" (these are offered according to the law), ⁹then he added, "Behold, I have come to do your will." He does away with the first in order to establish the second. ¹⁰And by that will we have been sanctified through the offering of the body of Jesus Christ once for all.

¹¹And every priest stands daily at his service, offering repeatedly the same sacrifices, which can never take away sins. ¹²But when Christ had offered for all time a single sacrifice for sins, he sat down at the right hand of God, ¹³waiting

> # Key Verse
>
> *Let us draw near with a true heart in full assurance of faith, with our hearts sprinkled clean from an evil conscience and our bodies washed with pure water* (Heb. 10:22).

be made a footstool for his feet. ¹⁴For by a single offering he has perfected for all time those who are being sanctified.

¹⁵And the Holy Spirit also bears witness to us; for after saying,

¹⁶"This is the covenant that I will
        make with them
    after those days, declares the
        Lord:
I will put my laws on their hearts,
    and write them on their
        minds,"
¹⁷then he adds,

"I will remember their sins
    and their lawless deeds
    no more."

¹⁸Where there is forgiveness of these, there is no longer any offering for sin.

Redemption Through the Blood of Christ

¹⁹Therefore, brothers, since we have confidence to enter the holy places by the blood of Jesus, ²⁰by the new and living way that he opened for us through the curtain, that is, through his flesh, ²¹and since we have a great priest over the house of God, ²²let us draw near with a true heart in full assurance of faith, with our hearts sprinkled clean from an evil conscience and our bodies washed

with pure water. ²³Let us hold fast the confession of our hope without wavering, for he who promised is faithful. ²⁴And let us consider how to stir up one another to love and good works, ²⁵not neglecting to meet together, as is the habit of some, but encouraging one another, and all the more as you see the Day drawing near.

²⁶For if we go on sinning deliberately after receiving the knowledge of the truth, there no longer remains a sacrifice for sins, ²⁷but a fearful expectation of judgment, and a fury of fire that will consume the adversaries. ²⁸Anyone who has set aside the law of Moses dies without mercy on the evidence of two or three witnesses. ²⁹How much worse punishment, do you think, will be deserved by the one who has spurned the Son of God, and has profaned the blood of the covenant by which he was sanctified, and has outraged the Spirit of grace? ³⁰For we know him who said, "Vengeance is mine; I will repay." And again, "The Lord will judge his people." ³¹It is a fearful thing to fall into the hands of the living God.

³²But recall the former days when, after you were enlightened, you endured a hard struggle with sufferings, ³³sometimes being publicly exposed to reproach and affliction, and sometimes being partners with those so treated. ³⁴For you had compassion on those in prison, and you joyfully accepted the plundering of your property, since you knew that you yourselves had a better possession and an abiding one. ³⁵Therefore do not throw away your confidence, which has a great reward. ³⁶For you have need of endurance, so that when you have done the will of God you may receive what is promised. ³⁷For,

> "Yet a little while,
>> and the coming one will
>>> come and will not delay;

> ³⁸but my righteous one shall live
>> by faith,
> and if he shrinks back,
> my soul has no pleasure in
>> him."

³⁹But we are not of those who shrink back and are destroyed, but of those who have faith and preserve their souls.

Go Deeper

The last section of Hebrews 10 expresses a significant and sober challenge. Verses 26–39 discuss the consequences that follow when a person has been exposed to all that God has declared and yet turns away to seek his or her own will. Such a person who continues "sinning deliberately" (v. 26) can expect worse judgment and punishment than those who deliberately turned away from the Law of Moses. The knowledge that could have led to their salvation becomes the cause of their condemnation. Why? Their attitude toward the Gospel has caused them to commit three grievous sins:

First, they have "spurned the Son of God" (v. 29). These are not people who "missed Jesus" by mistake. They saw Him and turned away, unwilling to let Him be their Savior. They have spurned the only One who could save them. The Greek word for this action is the same one Jesus used in Matthew 5:13 to describe what happens to salt that has lost its savor. It

(continued)

Go Deeper Continued . . .

is disregarded and trampled on. Treating Jesus that way means turning away from the only Way that can save.

Second, they have "profaned the blood of the covenant" (Heb. 10:29). The uniqueness and effectiveness of this blood was the subject of Hebrews 9:15–18 and 10:12–18. This is Christ's blood that has been treated as worthless (see Matt. 26:28; 1 Cor. 11:25).

Third, they have "outraged the Spirit of grace" (Heb. 10:29). Hebrews 9:14 reminds us of the intimate involvement of the Holy Spirit in Christ's sacrifice. It is God's Spirit that awakens us to the truth.

To wound the Holy Spirit (see Eph. 4:30) is a serious offense.

This combination of attitudes that dismiss Jesus goes a long way in explaining what Jesus meant when He said, "Therefore I tell you, every sin and blasphemy will be forgiven people, but the blasphemy against the Spirit will not be forgiven. And whoever speaks a word against the Son of Man will be forgiven, but whoever speaks against the Holy Spirit will not be forgiven, either in this age or in the age to come" (Matt. 12:31–32).

I n case we have missed the point, the writer of Hebrews now focuses his attention, in Hebrews 10:1–18, on the uniqueness of Jesus' sacrifice. It was unique in its character and unique in its effectiveness. There has never been another sacrifice like it, in which God Himself submitted to death on behalf of those He loves. And because the sacrifice was perfect, it required no repetition. Once was enough. "And by that will we have been sanctified through the offering of the body of Jesus Christ once for all" (v. 10).

The long history of the Old Covenant sacrifices down through the centuries was part of God's plan. But so were the details of Jesus' life and death. Jesus didn't come to earth to see how things would turn out, playing it by ear. He came to carry out His Father's will. We think of the cross as the vivid expression of God's love for us, but in many ways, the crucial point was when Jesus said to His Father in prayer hours before He endured the nails, "My Father, if it be possible, let this cup pass from me; nevertheless, not as I will, but as you will" (Matt. 26:39). It's not surprising, then, that the writer of Hebrews finds prophetic words about Jesus in the phrases of Psalm 40:6–8 (see Heb. 10:5–7), in particular the words, "I have come to do your will, O God" (v. 7).

> *"Jesus died once for us so that we could be free to live every day for God. He came to give us the abundant life."*

Jesus stands in stark contrast to the priests who presented the sacrifices over and over and over again. The repetition was itself a strong picture of captivity to sin. The freedom offered through the sacrifices was never lasting. Both priest and people realized even as they offered up one animal that they would soon return to offer another. We can almost see the writer shaking his head sadly as he wrote, "But in these sacrifices there is a reminder of sins every year" (v. 3). The Old Covenant begged for something better, and God supplied it in Jesus! That was the promise all along, for even in the years of the Old Covenant, God told His people that the New Covenant was coming (see vv. 16–17). Under the New Covenant, forgiveness would be offered based on the sacrifice already made.

Verse 19 begins with a typical application "therefore" in the Bible. We're about to be told how the preceding needs to be lived out. Note the two "since" and the three "let us" phrases that follow in verses 19–25. Since we have "confidence" (v. 19) and "a great high priest" (v. 21), we ought to take action. Our confidence and our leader are one and the same—Jesus. The word *confidence* comes from a Latin term that means "with faith." We tend to use it to express faith in ourselves, but here and always it should be based on faith in Jesus. Confidence in ourselves is bound to disappoint and fail; confidence in Christ is a sure thing!

The first application action resulting from this confidence is "let us draw near" (v. 22). The assurance of God's willingness to forgive ought to drive us to Him. James reminds us in a similar passage to "draw near to God, and he will draw near to you" (James 4:8). Instead of feeling forced to draw near in order to make sacrifices, we now have the freedom to draw near in worship and delight. The language of spiritual washing here reminds us of John's words, "If we confess our sins, he is faithful and just to forgive us our sins and to cleanse us from all unrighteousness" (1 John 1:9).

The second application action stemming from our confidence in Christ is "let us hold fast the confession of our hope" (Heb. 10:23). The previous "drawing near" is not so much an event in life but the direction of life. "Holding fast" means "staying on track and living out our assurance in Christ." Jesus died once for us so that we could be free to live every day for God. He came to give us the abundant life (see John 10:10).

The third application action is "let us consider how to stir up one another to love and good works" (Heb. 10:24). Isn't it amazing how often biblical teaching takes on the pattern of Jesus' point that everything boils down to the Great Commandment—loving God and loving our neighbors? The first two "let us" phrases had to do with the internal spiritual disciplines that express our love for God, our desire to draw near to Him continuously with heart, soul, mind and strength. This third "let us" phrase is a self-fulfilling counsel. The writer is provoking us to provoke one another to love and good works. There's something honoring in being thoughtfully provoked. When someone spends enough time thinking about us that they know just how to encourage and move us toward love and good deeds, they have valued us. Most of us know how to stir up people around us to things other than love and good works. This challenge may require a great deal of thought from us. And we can start by drawing near to God and letting Him direct our plans. This is living by faith!

Express It

The best way to consider how to stir or provoke others to love and good deeds is to pray for them. We can talk their situation over with God, thinking about ways in which we might encourage them and participate with them in what God wants to do in their lives.

Consider It

As you read Hebrews 10:1–39, consider these questions:

1) In what ways was the Law of Moses inadequate for the spiritual needs of people?

_____

_____

_____

2) What did the old sacrificial system accomplish?

_____

_____

_____

3) How does the writer of Hebrews 10 use Psalm 40:6–8 to explain an important idea about Jesus?

_____

_____

_____

4) How does Heb. 10:14 describe Jesus' ministry?

_____

_____

_____

5) According to verse 23, what is our primary motivation for remaining faithful?

_____

_____

_____

6) What examples can you think of when you or someone else stirred up a person to love and good deeds?

_____

_____

_____

7) How do verses 26–39 encourage you in your own spiritual life?

_____

_____

_____

The Great Relationship

Hebrews 11 is the great faith chapter in the New Testament. It has been called the Faith's Hall of Fame chapter. But it can also be seen as the chapter that highlights the great relationship we can have with God.

Hebrews 11:1–40

By Faith

11 Now faith is the assurance of things hoped for, the conviction of things not seen. ²For by it the people of old received their commendation. ³By faith we understand that the universe was created by the word of God, so that what is seen was not made out of things that are visible.

⁴By faith Abel offered to God a more acceptable sacrifice than Cain, through which he was commended as righteous, God commending him by accepting his gifts. And through his faith, though he died, he still speaks. ⁵By faith Enoch was taken up so that he should not see death, and he was not found, because God had taken him. Now before he was taken he was commended as having pleased God. ⁶And without faith it is impossible to please him, for whoever would draw near to God must believe that he exists and that he rewards those who seek him. ⁷By faith Noah, being warned by God concerning events as yet unseen, in reverent fear constructed an ark for the saving of his household. By this he condemned the world and became an heir of the righteousness that comes by faith.

⁸By faith Abraham obeyed when he was called to go out to a place that he was to receive as an inheritance. And he went out, not knowing where he was going. ⁹By faith he went to live in the land of promise, as in a foreign land, living in tents with Isaac and Jacob, heirs with him of the same promise. ¹⁰For he was looking forward to the city that has foundations, whose designer and builder is God. ¹¹By faith Sarah herself received power to conceive, even when she was past the age, since she considered him faithful who had promised. ¹²Therefore from one man, and him as good as dead, were born

> # Key Verse
>
> *And without faith it is impossible to please him, for whoever would draw near to God must believe that he exists and that he rewards those who seek him* (Heb. 11:6).

descendants as many as the stars of heaven and as many as the innumerable grains of sand by the seashore.

¹³These all died in faith, not having received the things promised, but having seen them and greeted them from afar, and having acknowledged that they were strangers and exiles on the earth. ¹⁴For people who speak thus make it clear that they are seeking a homeland. ¹⁵If they had been thinking of that land from which they had gone out, they would have had opportunity to return. ¹⁶But as it is, they desire a better country, that is, a heavenly one. Therefore God is not ashamed to be called their God, for he has prepared for them a city.

¹⁷By faith Abraham, when he was tested, offered up Isaac, and he who had received the promises was in the act of offering up his only son, ¹⁸of whom it was said, "Through Isaac shall your offspring be named." ¹⁹He considered that God was able even to raise him from the dead, from which, figuratively speaking, he did receive him back. ²⁰By faith Isaac invoked future blessings on Jacob and Esau. ²¹By faith Jacob, when dying, blessed each of the sons of Joseph, bowing in worship over the head of his staff. ²²By faith Joseph, at the end of his

life, made mention of the exodus of the Israelites and gave directions concerning his bones.

²³By faith Moses, when he was born, was hidden for three months by his parents, because they saw that the child was beautiful, and they were not afraid of the king's edict. ²⁴By faith Moses, when he was grown up, refused to be called the son of Pharaoh's daughter, ²⁵choosing rather to be mistreated with the people of God than to enjoy the fleeting pleasures of sin. ²⁶He considered the reproach of Christ greater wealth than the treasures of Egypt, for he was looking to the reward. ²⁷By faith he left Egypt, not being afraid of the anger of the king, for he endured as seeing him who is invisible. ²⁸By faith he kept the Passover and sprinkled the blood, so that the Destroyer of the firstborn might not touch them.

²⁹By faith the people crossed the Red Sea as on dry land, but the Egyptians, when they attempted to do the same, were drowned. ³⁰By faith the walls of Jericho fell down after they had been encircled for seven days. ³¹By faith Rahab the prostitute did not perish with those who were disobedient, because she had given a friendly welcome to the spies.

³²And what more shall I say? For time would fail me to tell of Gideon, Barak, Samson, Jephthah, of David and Samuel and the prophets—³³who through faith conquered kingdoms, enforced justice, obtained promises, stopped the mouths of lions, ³⁴quenched the power of fire, escaped the edge of the sword, were made strong out of weakness, became mighty in war, put foreign armies to flight. ³⁵Women received back their dead by resurrection. Some were tortured, refusing to accept release, so that they might rise again to a better life. ³⁶Others suffered mocking and flogging, and even chains and imprisonment. ³⁷They were stoned, they were sawn in two, they were killed with the sword. They went about in skins of sheep and goats, destitute, afflicted, mistreated—³⁸of whom the world was not worthy—wandering about in deserts and mountains, and in dens and caves of the earth.

³⁹And all these, though commended through their faith, did not receive what was promised, ⁴⁰since God had provided something better for us, that apart from us they should not be made perfect.

Go Deeper

Reading Hebrews 11 in a Bible with a good cross-reference system will give you many opportunities to flip back to the Old Testament for the context of the lives listed in this chapter. This can be an interesting exercise, because the background of many of these faith heroes reminds us they were very "human" and surprisingly like us. Yet they lived by faith, just as we need to do. Coming after all the writer says about the

improvements on the Old Covenant that we find in the New Covenant, we need to remember that the heroes in chapter 11 were not people who were accepted by God because they lived up to the Old Covenant. They were people who were accepted by God through faith, just as we are. The cross was just as necessary for those who lived by faith thousands of years before Jesus as it is for those of us who live by faith thousands of years

(continued)

afterwards! They trusted that God would find a way for them; we trust that God has found a way for us. Jesus is always and has always been the Way. Without Jesus, faith is little more than wishful thinking.

One of the advantages we have over these Old Testament saints is that we get to exercise a more informed faith. Job said, "Though he slay me, I will hope in him" (Job 13:15). Isaiah was only one of many who said, "Behold, God is my salvation; I will trust, and will not be afraid" (Isa. 12:2). We can have the same kind of relationship with God they had, but we are more fully aware of how God has made salvation possible. We can say, along with the apostle Paul, "I have been crucified with Christ. It is no longer I who live, but Christ who lives in me. And the life I now live in the flesh I live by faith in the Son of God, who loved me and gave himself for me" (Gal. 2:20).

T he writer of Hebrews introduced the list of the famous faithful with some significant notes about faith. He understood that it was even more important to remember the God who inspired the faith of the ancients than it was to remember the inspiring faith of the ancients. Right from the beginning, this chapter is directed toward us. The previous chapter was filled with encouragement to live by faith; this chapter defines the faith by which we should live. By looking at the relationship that others have had with God, we are invited to examine and commit ourselves to a similar relationship with our Heavenly Father.

In fact, this chapter of Hebrews helps us answer three significant questions about a relationship with God: (1) Is a relationship with God possible? (2) Is a relationship with God desirable, something someone would want to have? (3) Is a relationship with God attainable?

Let's first look at questions 1 and 2. We live in a world in which relationships are made nearly every day and broken nearly every day. Is it possible to have a relationship with God? If we look at Hebrews 11, the answer seems to be *yes*. Is a relationship with God desirable? There are a lot of people who say, "No, a relationship with God is not something I want." Self-sufficient people, for example, say, "I don't need God. Why would I need a relationship with Him?" "The fool says

> *"Our role in God's plan may not be as dramatic as the part played by the famous faithful, but we are still called to the same kind of faith."*

in his heart, 'There is no God'" (Ps. 14:1). So, there are people who do say they desire no relationship at all with God.

But imagine for a moment what it would be like to have a relationship with the God who reveals Himself in the Bible and through Jesus Christ. Imagine being loved at all times. Imagine being loved unconditionally, having not met prior conditions or having been the "right kind" of person for God to love. Imagine knowing Someone who always does what is best for you, Someone who makes sure that all things work together for good to those who love God, to those who are called according to His purpose (see Rom. 8:28). Imagine God's unwavering faithfulness. He is Someone who would never take advantage of you or lie to you. Imagine the wisest, wealthiest, most powerful person in the world. Would having a relationship with that kind of person be desirable? Except for the atheist, the fool, and the self-sufficient person, most of us would respond, "Yes, having a relationship with that kind of person certainly is desirable."

If having a relationship with God is desirable, then the question becomes, "Is it possible?" Some people think of God's divine nature (so unapproachable, so unattainable, so sovereign) and conclude a relationship is impossible. And they are right—unless God wants such a relationship! If God is God, then He can do (and did) what is necessary to make a relationship with Him possible. Remember Jesus' words the last night before the cross: "And this is eternal life, that they know you the only true God, and Jesus Christ whom you have sent" (John 17:3). There's the possibility of relationship!

We still have to answer the third question, "Is a relationship with God attainable?" If it is possible, then how do you attain it? Jesus is God's answer to this question. Both John 3:16 and Luke 19:10 talk about God's action to make a relationship with Him attainable.

Hebrews 11:6 tells us that without faith it is impossible to please God, but with faith it is possible for us to have a relationship with God through His Son, Jesus Christ, the Savior. We do this by placing our faith in what He did at Calvary, when He died for our sins to be all that God required to pay the penalty for our sins. Psalm 37:3–5 describes the trusting character of our relationship with God. Notice how many times the word *trust* occurs in those verses. The kind of relationship that you want with God is one in which you have Someone in whom you can trust. That's the kind of practical, day-by-day faith that marked the lives of those people listed in Hebrews 11.

Relationships in this world unfortunately tend not to last very long. That's a painful part of living in a fallen world. But when we have a relationship with God, it's not going to stop. It's not going to last for ten years or just a lifetime. God says to us, "I have loved you with an everlasting love" (Jer. 31:3). That means the relationship with God started long before we were born, and it will go on long after we are in glory. When you and I have a relationship with God, it is an everlasting relationship. There's nothing that can separate us from the love of God in Christ Jesus (see Rom. 8:38–39).

Our role in God's plan may not be as dramatic as the part played by the famous faithful, but we are still called to the same kind of faith. As you read through those lives in Hebrews 11, the point is not to be impressed by their faith but to be encouraged in ours! We, too, can live in a great faith relationship with God—it's possible, desirable, and attainable—by His grace.

Express It

It's easy to see how often the phrase "by faith" is repeated throughout Hebrews 11. Perhaps we need to bring that pattern into our prayer lives sometimes. As you pray the next time, think about ways to state your concerns, thoughts, and requests to God by faith. Use the phrase often as a reminder that prayer is a very personal expression of trust in God.

Consider It

As you read Hebrews 11:1–40, consider these questions:

1) What is faith and how does Hebrews 11 help you understand it?

2) How does faith affect your relationship with God?

3) What characteristics did the faith of these famous faithful have in common?

4) How do patience and endurance affect our understanding of faith?

5) With which of the people in this chapter would you most enjoy a conversation? Why?

6) Explain the summary statement about faithful people "of whom the world was not worthy" (v. 38)?

7) In what areas of your life do you recognize special opportunities to exercise faith right now?

The Ultimate Mediator

Reading history is like watching others live their lives. But what if the situation were reversed? What if our examples from the past could see us and were cheering us on to do our very best in the race of life? They can't, but their lives can certainly be an example to us! Would we live differently if we thought God was expecting us to learn from those who have lived before our time?

Hebrews 12:1-29

The Time of the End

12 Therefore, since we are surrounded by so great a cloud of witnesses, let us also lay aside every weight, and sin which clings so closely, and let us run with endurance the race that is set before us, ²looking to Jesus, the founder and perfecter of our faith, who for the joy that was set before him endured the cross, despising the shame, and is seated at the right hand of the throne of God.

Do Not Grow Weary

³Consider him who endured from sinners such hostility against himself, so that you may not grow weary or fainthearted. ⁴In your struggle against sin you have not yet resisted to the point of shedding your blood. ⁵And have you forgotten the exhortation that addresses you as sons?

> "My son, do not regard lightly
> the discipline of the Lord,
> nor be weary when reproved
> by him.
> ⁶For the Lord disciplines the one
> he loves,
> and chastises every son whom
> he receives."

⁷It is for discipline that you have to endure. God is treating you as sons. For what son is there whom his father does not discipline? ⁸If you are left without discipline, in which all have participated, then you are illegitimate children and not sons. ⁹Besides this, we have had earthly fathers who disciplined us and we respected them. Shall we not much more be subject to the Father of spirits and live? ¹⁰For they disciplined us for a short time as it seemed best to them, but he disciplines us for our good, that we may share his holiness. ¹¹For the moment all discipline seems painful rather than

---

Key Verse

"Looking to Jesus, the founder and perfecter of our faith, who for the joy that was set before him endured the cross, despising the shame, and is seated at the right hand of the throne of God" (Heb. 12:2).

---

pleasant, but later it yields the peaceful fruit of righteousness to those who have been trained by it.

¹²Therefore lift your drooping hands and strengthen your weak knees, ¹³and make straight paths for your feet, so that what is lame may not be put out of joint but rather be healed. ¹⁴Strive for peace with everyone, and for the holiness without which no one will see the Lord. ¹⁵See to it that no one fails to obtain the grace of God; that no "root of bitterness" springs up and causes trouble, and by it many become defiled; ¹⁶that no one is sexually immoral or unholy like Esau, who sold his birthright for a single meal. ¹⁷For you know that afterward, when he desired to inherit the blessing, he was rejected, for he found no chance to repent, though he sought it with tears.

A Kingdom That Cannot Be Shaken

¹⁸For you have not come to what may be touched, a blazing fire and darkness and gloom and a tempest ¹⁹and the sound of a trumpet and a voice whose words made the hearers beg that no further messages be spoken to them. ²⁰For they could not endure the order that

was given, "If even a beast touches the mountain, it shall be stoned." ²¹Indeed, so terrifying was the sight that Moses said, "I tremble with fear." ²²But you have come to Mount Zion and to the city of the living God, the heavenly Jerusalem, and to innumerable angels in festal gathering, ²³and to the assembly of the firstborn who are enrolled in heaven, and to God, the judge of all, and to the spirits of the righteous made perfect, ²⁴and to Jesus, the mediator of a new covenant, and to the sprinkled blood that speaks a better word than the blood of Abel.

²⁵See that you do not refuse him who is speaking. For if they did not escape when they refused him who warned them on earth, much less will we escape if we reject him who warns from heaven. ²⁶At that time his voice shook the earth, but now he has promised, "Yet once more I will shake not only the earth but also the heavens." ²⁷This phrase, "Yet once more," indicates the removal of things that are shaken—that is, things that have been made—in order that the things that cannot be shaken may remain. ²⁸Therefore let us be grateful for receiving a kingdom that cannot be shaken, and thus let us offer to God acceptable worship, with reverence and awe, ²⁹for our God is a consuming fire.

Go Deeper

One way to think about Hebrews 12 is to call it a "let us" salad. In the following list, the occurrences of the "let us" phrase (either directly or by implication) give us a specific action to undertake each time it is mentioned.

Let us lay aside every weight (v. 1).

(Let us) lay aside every sin (v. 1).

Let us run (v. 1).

(Let us) consider him (v. 3).

(Let us) lift [our] drooping hands (v. 12).

(Let us) strengthen [our] weak knees (v. 12).

(Let us) make straight paths (v. 13).

(Let us) strive for peace with everyone (v. 14).

(Let us) see to it that no one fails to obtain the grace of God (v. 15).

Let us be grateful (v. 28).

Let us offer to God acceptable worship (v. 28).

Take some time to write down what each of these actions would mean in your life right now. As you read the verses around each of these "let us" statements, notice how they build toward becoming less about us and more about others and then about God. Put into practice what God shows you.

Audiences can *spectate* or participate. They can be casual or even bored observers, but they can also greatly influence the action on the field. They can encourage or discourage performers. When the writer of Hebrews was finished with his review of Old Testament faith-heroes, he presented them to us as a "cloud of witnesses" (Heb. 12:1), a huge audience, a band of believers who set high the bar of faith, urging on by their example those who presently occupy the field of life. He was referring to the witness of history, the testimony of lives that have gone before ours. Their examples cheer us on like a crowd. This is another "therefore" passage, in which the writer tells us it's time to move from the lesson to the application.

When it comes to keywords, *also* often provides a crucial clue to application. In Hebrews 12:1, the writer points out that our "witnesses" have been where we are and that we can "also" do what they did. This involves not only laying aside sin and weights but also running the life-race laid out in front of us (v. 1). Our attention must be on Christ—"the founder and perfecter of our faith" (v. 2). This means Jesus plants faith in us and brings it to maturity. He's the source and object of our faith. And the way He handled the cross makes this clear.

In the thinking of Hebrews 12, the danger to our faith isn't persecution or death. The greater risk comes from our tendency to become "weary or fainthearted" (v. 3). We don't fail to run the race because it gets too hard; we fail because we think it's too long. In a world that craves instant gratification more and more, the disciplines of discipleship don't sound like a quick enough process. Like fast food, we want fast faith, fast discipleship, fast maturity, and fast rewards. But how often do we stop to realize that the short-lived satisfaction that comes from fast food might be the same result that would come from spiritual shortcuts? Faith, discipleship, and maturity all take time to grow. Attempts to bring them about quickly result in people who are "weary or fainthearted" (v. 3).

The phrase "looking to Jesus" means following Him. When Jesus asked His disciples to follow Him, He didn't put a time limit on His request. Following Him is a no-turning-back proposition. In fact, He

"The challenges in the Christian life come back not to our ability or strength but to Christ's. It's not, in the end, about us; it's about Him. . . . He is the Way as well as the One who leads us on the way."

doesn't want us to use even the experiences of other believers or His plans for them when we are responding to His plans for us. During Peter's last conversation with Jesus (see John 21:15–22), the Lord gave Peter some affirming instructions and then reminded him, "Follow me" (John 21:19). Peter noticed that John was close by, so he asked Jesus, "Lord, what about this man?" (John 21:21). Jesus heard the question but also heard the motive behind it—a desire to compare. He told Peter, "If it is my will that he remain until I come, what is that to you? You follow me!" (John 21:22). For the growing disciple of Jesus, it's not as important to track how long we have been following Him as it is to make sure we are following now, today.

The pattern Jesus set was endurance. Note how this word *endurance* shows up in Hebrews 12:1–3, 7. Twice it's used to describe Jesus and twice to describe how we are expected to follow Him. The fact that we will have to endure is itself a mark of God's fatherly care for us. He wants to "grow us up" into His children, so He uses discipline along the way. As always in this grand book, the challenges in the Christian life come back not to our ability or strength but to Christ's. It's not, in the end, about us; it's about Him. We follow Him because He makes following possible. He is the great mediator. He is the Way as well as the One who leads us on the way.

By the time we get to verse 18 in this chapter, we are back to remembering the scope of God's character and unshakable kingdom into which we have been called as citizens. All the glimpses of God's majesty and awesome power that we get in the Old Testament pointed to the "mediator of a new covenant" (v. 24), Jesus. This is one of those places in the New Testament where we get some hint of what Jesus may have told the two disciples as they walked on the road to Emmaus on Resurrection morning and the Lord "interpreted to them in all the Scriptures the things concerning himself" (Luke 24:27). Through Christ we are citizens of a kingdom that cannot be shaken and subjects of a king who is King of kings. No wonder a chapter that begins in a huge stadium of witnesses ends with worship, for we get to join with the great cloud of witnesses in offering thanks and praise to God.

Express It

We discover in this chapter that challenges in a Christian's life can be intense but can also seem long and drawn out. We can respond with growth or with bitterness to God's discipline and training. Take some time in prayer to examine how you've been doing lately. Ask God's Spirit to point out ways in which you may be developing spiritual weariness or faintheartedness. Reclaim your citizenship in Christ's Kingdom!

Consider It

As you read Hebrews 12:1-29, consider these questions:

1) Of what event or circumstance does the opening of this chapter remind you?

_____

_____

_____

2) When we are disciplined by God, what does this chapter tell us that means?

_____

_____

_____

3) How much can we discover about Jesus from this chapter?

_____

_____

_____

4) How would you use these verses to explain God's holiness?

_____

_____

_____

5) What does it mean in your daily life that you are a member of Christ's unshakable kingdom?

_____

_____

_____

6) How do you handle spiritual weariness or faintheartedness?

_____

_____

_____

7) In what ways does this chapter drive you to a deeper desire to worship God?

_____

_____

_____

Old Tradition, New Savior

Many people keep two sets of objectives for their lives—the public ones and the private ones. The public ones can be talked about; the private ones remain hidden. But it is these latter ones that drive our decisions. How similar are your lists?

Hebrews 13:1–25

Sacrifices Pleasing to God

13 Let brotherly love continue. [2]Do not neglect to show hospitality to strangers, for thereby some have entertained angels unawares. [3]Remember those who are in prison, as though in prison with them, and those who are mistreated, since you also are in the body. [4]Let marriage be held in honor among all, and let the marriage bed be undefiled, for God will judge the sexually immoral and adulterous. [5]Keep your life free from love of money, and be content with what you have, for he has said, "I will never leave you nor forsake you." [6]So we can confidently say,

"The Lord is my helper;
I will not fear;
what can man do to me?"

[7]Remember your leaders, those who spoke to you the word of God. Consider the outcome of their way of life, and imitate their faith. [8]Jesus Christ is the same yesterday and today and forever. [9]Do not be led away by diverse and strange teachings, for it is good for the heart to be strengthened by grace, not by foods, which have not benefited those devoted to them. [10]We have an altar from which those who serve the tent have no right to eat. [11]For the bodies of those animals whose blood is brought into the holy places by the high priest as a sacrifice for sin are burned outside the camp. [12]So Jesus also suffered outside the gate in order to sanctify the people through his own blood. [13]Therefore let us go to him outside the camp and bear the reproach he endured. [14]For here we have no lasting city, but we seek the city that is to come. [15]Through him then let us continually offer up a sacrifice of praise to God, that is, the fruit of lips that acknowledge his name. [16]Do not neglect to do good and to share what you have, for such sacrifices are pleasing to God.

> # Key Verse
>
> *Keep your life free from love of money, and be content with what you have, for he has said, "I will never leave you nor forsake you"* (Heb. 13:5).

[17]Obey your leaders and submit to them, for they are keeping watch over your souls, as those who will have to give an account. Let them do this with joy and not with groaning, for that would be of no advantage to you.

[18]Pray for us, for we are sure that we have a clear conscience, desiring to act honorably in all things. [19]I urge you the more earnestly to do this in order that I may be restored to you the sooner.

Benediction

[20]Now may the God of peace who brought again from the dead our Lord Jesus, the great shepherd of the sheep, by the blood of the eternal covenant, [21]equip you with everything good that you may do his will, working in us that which is pleasing in his sight, through Jesus Christ, to whom be glory forever and ever. Amen.

Final Greetings

[22]I appeal to you, brothers, bear with my word of exhortation, for I have written to you briefly. [23]You should know that our brother Timothy has been released, with whom I shall see you if he comes soon. [24]Greet all your leaders and all the saints. Those who come from Italy send you greetings. [25]Grace be with all of you.

Go Deeper

Let's look briefly at several other passages of Scripture that demonstrate how the Bible encourages contentment and equates craving with a variety of traits that are not positive. In other words, if you and I can't control our cravings, it will lead us to something far more serious than just craving.

In 1 Timothy 6:6–10 the apostle Paul equates craving with temptation. Contentment will keep you from temptation because if you aren't content with what you have, you will fall into the temptation of the rich—to do anything you can to get more.

Jesus told a parable in Luke 12:15–21 to illustrate how craving leads to short-sighted decisions and coveting. The rich farmer gave no thought to thanksgiving but only to his wants and comfort. We need to evaluate our lives by God's stunning judgment of the farmer: "God said to him: 'Fool! This night your soul is required of you, and the things you have prepared, whose will they be?' So is the one who lays up treasure for himself and is not rich toward God" (Luke 12:20–21).

Philippians 4:8–14 lists an amazing assortment of mental exercises other than craving that ought to occupy our time and energy. Paul reminds us here that contentment is learned! And it's learned through Christ who strengthens us.

In 2 Corinthians 9:5–11 Paul points to the crucial role of giving in the process of contentment. Craving leads to hoarding; contentment leads to sharing. And sharing is ultimately fulfilling in a way that hoarding can never be. Giving is the best way to remind ourselves who we really trust!

Some years ago, a survey was conducted by the American Council on Education that found that 75 percent of 200,000 incoming college freshmen reported that being financially well off was an essential in life. As they began their academic careers, their goal in life was to make money. They actually equated being financially well-off with being happy. Subsequent research showed that, though many of these students succeeded in achieving wealth at an early age, they did not find the happiness they were expecting. In the final chapter of Hebrews, the writer reviewed his teaching and gave some final words of encouragement.

> **"***The presence of the Lord Jesus in our lives is the help that we need in order to be content. . . . Our ultimate worthy want is God, and what He wants for us. We can be truly content with nothing else.***"**

Hebrews takes the long view of the Christian life. The practical suggestions in this book have to do with the big picture and life-long disciplines. This writer wasn't offering quick-fix spiritual answers to his readers. He wanted them to realize God was involved with them in a process that would require all of life. In this way, he joins the chorus of the rest of the New Testament in offering counsel for basic discipleship. One of the central themes in this chapter, for instance, is contentment. Because of the New Covenant established in Christ, we have the best reasons to be content.

The letter to the Hebrews certainly has a message for today. The central Bible teaching on contentment reveals perhaps why the Church has so little impact on the world today. When those outside the kingdom look at our lives, do they see contentment or do they see the same earth-centered traits that saturate their own lives? Do they see boredom, dissatisfaction, and cravings that grow in places where contentment has been rejected? In fact, one of the terms the Bible uses frequently as a contrast to contentment is *craving* (see Go Deeper).

Craving is not the way for Christians to live when we are under a better covenant, because God has a better way. His method, which is better than craving, is called "contentment." Here again, it's necessary to bring the mirror of God's Word up to the reality of our lives. If so many Christians know about God's invitation to contentment, then why do so few Christians live contented lives?

When we meet people today who are truly content, we often wonder, *What's wrong with them?* We are so filled with discontentment that contentment appears to be some kind of denial or ignorance. Perhaps we should be asking, "What's wrong with us?"

For Christians living in poor countries, the issue of contentment is a fact of life. They have to be content with what they have because that's often all there is. They deal with the reality that even basic needs may not be met. We deal constantly with a mind-boggling and soul-polluting cascade of abundance. Every day we are bombarded with attempts to convince us that all sorts of luxuries we might want are actually things we need. If we are not content, we are extremely vulnerable to advertising. But we can learn to be content with the things that we have if we are not constantly craving something more, something newer, and something larger. Contentment has to do with temporary needs (see 1 Tim. 6:8). We develop and deepen contentment when our wants no longer determine our decisions and attitudes. One of the first steps in learning contentment is reminding ourselves regularly that we never have to have our wants. If we get our attitudes right, we're going to have the right response to our situation in life.

But we do have to make a distinction between being content in Christ and being content with things as they are. The Bible doesn't give us any reason for not seeking to change bad things. We should always want to make situations better, particularly for others. Contentment doesn't mean we stop caring. The problem many of us have is that we care most deeply about our wants rather than about the needs of others. We can counteract this tendency by learning to give, because contentment comes only through a heart that's full. And, ironically, a fullness of heart comes only when we are giving more often than we are receiving. We develop contentment by practicing how to give away the things we have—not the junk in our lives, not the things we don't need—but to give away time, energy, and things—possessions that we have that perhaps someone else can use more than we can. Such decisions contribute to an attitude of contentment.

Christ tells us He will be our helper in this process (see Heb. 13:6). The presence of the Lord Jesus in our lives is the help that we need in order to be content. The key verse in Hebrews 13 provides us with a statement from God: "I will never leave you nor forsake you." As long as we think that anything or anyone is more desirable than God's presence in our lives, we will never discover the freedom of contentment. Our ultimate worthy want is God and what He wants for us. We can be truly content with nothing else.

Express It

From time to time, practice a "giving prayer." Ask God to bring to mind things and ways you can give to others. When He helps you think of items, make a list and follow through. The exercise of breaking your ties with things will be healthy. Meditate on the significance of "God loves a cheerful giver" (2 Cor. 9:7).

Consider It

As you read Hebrews 13:1–25, consider these questions:

1) In what ways does the issue of contentment come up in this chapter?

_____

_____

_____

2) How many specific commands can you find in this chapter? How many of them apply to your life directly?

_____

_____

_____

3) How is the significance of spiritual leadership highlighted in this chapter?

_____

_____

_____

4) What claims does this chapter make about Jesus? How are they significant?

_____

_____

_____

5) How do verses 11–15 illustrate again the unique sacrifice of Jesus?

_____

_____

_____

6) What single verse in this chapter presents you with the greatest challenge?

_____

_____

_____

7) Read the benediction in verses 20–21. How does it summarize the Letter to the Hebrews?

_____

_____

_____

Notes

Notes